REMEDIAL VAASTU
for Shops, Offices and Industries

Dr. N. H. Sahasrabuddhe
M.E. (I.I.Sc.) F.I.V. Ph.D.

Gautami N. Sahasrabuddhe
Software Consultant & Vaastu Pandit

STERLING PUBLISHERS (P) LTD.
Regd. Office: A1/256 Safdarjung Enclave,
New Delhi-110029. Cin: U22110DL1964PTC211907
Phone: +91 82877 98380
e-mail: mail@sterlingpublishers.in
www.sterlingpublishers.in

Remedial Vaastu for Shops, Offices and Industries
© 2019, Dr. N. H. Sahasrabuddhe
ISBN 978 81 207 8366 9
First Edition - 2013
Reprint - 2019

All rights are reserved.
No part of this publication may be reproduced, stored in a retrieval system or transmitted, in any form or by any means, mechanical, photocopying, recording or otherwise, without prior written permission of the author.

Printed in India

Printed and Published by Sterling Publishers Pvt. Ltd.,
Plot No. 13, Ecotech-III, Greater Noida - 201306,
Uttar Pradesh, India

With love and respect I dedicate this book to
"Guruji Sri Sri Ravishankar"
Founder,
The Art of Living Foundation
and
Ved Vidnyan Maha Vidyapeeth
whose divine support inspires and guides us in life.

Preface

Comprehensive perception is the beginning to understand the nature of Eastern oriental sciences. A sacred thread that connects man to nature is the core of oriental theme. A search for peace, progress and prosperity on various levels of existence, is a by-product of search for the soul and nature. Since this search is divine, its reflection has given a positive dimension to human life.

A fact is a physical phenomenon but the thought is an organic matter that connects the self to the world. Mind and thought are dimensioned, directed and developed on the quality of breath, which depends on many outer and inner aspects. Oriental sciences have this multidimensional approach—when it speaks of mind, it speaks of water element and it may speak of position of moon in the sky, along with the entire reflection of relation of cosmic and individual breath. When it speaks of fire, it may hint to the east zone extending the awareness to the qualities of Mars, along with the entire reflection of self and relation to the society. This comprehensive perception of the fact makes it a multiphenomenal, living entity of life.

Constraints, choice and freedom are like self-contradictory terms but nature contains all these things without any antagonism. That is, the power of Nature. When you search for discipline in the laws of Nature, it may show its theory of choice and the rule of least efforts. So the order of nature is built on many multidisciplinary modules of odd diversities. All these things are very nicely explained in "Darshan Shastra" while defining the *Aatma* (Soul), *Prakriti* (Order) and *Srushti* (Outer Order).

Length, area and volume are interdependent but their qualities are changing with the ratio-proportions. Quality is an organic entity whereas L x B x D are physical phenomenal factors. This is known as *Gun-vad* in the traditional scriptures.

All systems have different ratio-proportion for their survival. The optimum ratio is such that works with minimum friction. Here one enters in the dynamics of time, event, self and existence.

The entire oriental science is standing on the boundaries of life and death, time and directions, living and non-living, energy and matter so its scope one may find odd, if he has not understood the way to know it or developed an eye that connects life and death, energy and matter, etc.

Industrial structures are reflection of science, development and social movement. This book focuses on these factors through the study of proportions, gradients, dimensions, directions, five great elements and eventology. Alignment with the energy streams and organisation of five great elements are the main issues of Vaastu Shastra.

This book is a practical guide to know the successful forms of industrial structures derived from studies conducted on several existing factories and industries. These forms have been developed after conformation with the constraints of traditional Vaastu Shastra and are based on the laws of environmental engineering and climatology.

Industrial patterns are changing rapidly. The face of the market is ambiguous and leads to lack of knowledge of trends and patterns. Uncertainty has created many voids that hinder conformity and creativity. Here an attempt has been made to find the solutions.

Astrology speaks of *time*. Vaastu speaks of *directions*. Eventology speaks of *time and directions* simultaneously. Presented here is a correlation of the concepts of Astrology to those of Vaastu to ultimately examine the scope of eventology and happening.

N. H. Sahasrabuddhe
dr.nhs.vaastu@gmail.com
09822011050/020-25531989.

Contents

	Preface	v
1.	Business Vaastu	1
2.	Spaces: Wombs of Creation	5
3.	Environmental Aspect	8
4.	Earth Elemental Aspect	12
5.	Energy Elemental Aspect	16
6.	Success, Failure and Liquidation	21
7.	Classification of Industries	27
8.	Matrix of Space, Time and Events	31
9.	Ideal Industrial Planning	35

   a. Two-stream Theory
   b. Five Great Elements
   c. Planetary identification
   d. Forms, weights and loads
   e. Roofing Patterns
   f. Ratio proportion
   g. Planning the gates, entrances and doors
   h. Natural site selections.
   i. Energy, Axis and form
   j. Magnetic asymmetry
   k. Climate and Environment
   l. Travel of light.

10. Miracles and Reality   63
11. Cosmic Remedies of Eight Directions   86
    a. East Zone
    b. Southeast Zone
    c. South Zone
    d. Southwest Zone
    e. West Zone
    f. Northwest Zone
    g. North Zone
    h. Northeast zone
12. Cosmic Remedies   104
    a. North Zone
    b. East Zone
    c. West Zone
    d. South Zone
    e. Northeast Zone
    f. Southeast Zone
    g. Southwest Zone
    h. Northwest Zone
13. Forms of Sacred Geometry   117
    a. Cylindrical Forms
    b. Lean to Roof
    c. Lantern effects in ceiling
    d. Ideal Form
14. Software Industry and Call Centres   128
    a. People with the sun signs Aries, Leo and Sagittarius
    b. People with the sun signs Taurus, Virgo and Capricorn
    c. People with the sun signs Gemini, Libra and Aquarius

  d. People with the sun signs Cancer, Scorpio and Pisces
  e. Nine Remedies
    i. Natural light
    ii. Central breathing zones
    iii. "C-forms" opening to North and East
    iv. Terraces to North and East
    v. Golden ratio
    vi. Fish Ponds and Water bodies
    vii. Use of Pyramidal Ceilings
    viii. Colours
    ix. Table Tops

15. Astro Vaastu Concepts (Period of Red Alert)   144
  a. Five Great Elements
  b. Source and Sink
  c. Axis
  d. Planets
  e. Cycles of Nature
  f. Theory of Astro Vaastu
  g. River to South
  h. River to West
  i. Temporary Essential Remedies
  j. North Zone
  l. South Zone
  m. East Zone
  n. West Zone

16. Hospitals and Nursing Homes   157
  a. North Zone
  b. Northeast Zone
  c. East Zone
  d. Southeast Zone

  e. South Zone
  f. Southwest Zone
  g. West Zone
  h. Northwest Zone
17. Shops, Malls and Stores   164
  a. North Zone
  b. East Zone
  c. South Zone
  d. West Zone
  f. Sub-directions

Conclusion   174

1

BUSINESS VAASTU

It is a public place where many social elements and public interest are related to each other. One successful industry can change the face of an entire surrounding. In Maharashtra one can trace such examples through the co-operative movement and its reflection in sugar industry. Telco and Bajaj have supported innumerable small-scale units in surrounding industrial estates. Hence one successful industrial mega model can play a significant role in the development of a country. Simultaneously, failure of certain industrial estates has led to huge losses of public funds and assets, e.g. Enron, Kurkumbh and Mahad estate. In Kurkumbh Industrial estate on Solapur national highway, around 60% industrial units are closed, whereas in Mahad estate, 80% small-scale units are closed. One dying industrial unit deprives hundreds of families of their daily bread and supports the sinking of an industrial movement. Success of an industry depends on many aspects. It is very difficult to define a formula for success of any industry. Leadership, utility, demand, labour involvement, political support, availability of basic material, ever-changing frame of time and science, etc. are certain static and dynamic factors, related to a successful industrial unit. These factors can affect the success independently and interdependently both. Any logical effort to define elements of success is futile due to the presence of various elements of success. In many cases, even if one of the above elements has affected success and vice versa presence of all other positive elements has led to failure. Success is similar to a musical concert where one string of violin can destruct the harmony of the musical composition. Logical search and thinking leads to involvement of supernatural elements in the organics of success. This failure of logic and thought processes ignites the hunt in different planes of existence, which are beyond the realm of analysis and theories. Order of nature and its cyclic pattern becomes the first medium of enquiry to search the pattern of life. Different rhythms in dynamic continuum with befitting equilibrium are the truth of Nature. It is a mega system that accommodates the irregularities of all existing systems without irruption and complaints. There are two systems of understanding to anything; one system starts from whole to part, which is an Eastern comprehensive system. In this system reflection of order of Nature through rhythm is analysed without any break and cuts of system. The other system starts from "part to whole", which is a Western scientific system. In this system, a smallest micro unit is analyzed on an individual basic.

Innumerable elements are involved in defining the success of any unit. Time, accessibility, availability and utility are the important factors, which play an important role in the success of any unit. It has been observed that though all the factors are favourable still the product does not click. Management, administration and advertising have played effective roles in the success of a unit, but this success does not last long and then the question of some mystic element comes into play. In this book we are going to search for some module, which has not failed on the cosmic platform. The research for this module has been done through the studies of basic Vaastu Shastra and through the analysis of many existing case studies on practical ground. Enormous data on failures of many industries form the basis of all conclusions given in this book. Almost every case conforms to the theory of traditional Vaastu Shastra through various aspects related to directions, five great elements, energy streams, materials, effect of planets, movement and classifications of actions related to productions, type of product, loads, volumes and surroundings, etc. Some sample cases of variety of products are discussed in this book, so that a reader gets an overall idea of effectiveness of this ancient science. Author is conscious of the positive fact of requirement of 21st century. The international ground is an indefinite challenge and complexity of the subject is unlimited. Being an engineer by profession, the author has complete focus on factors related to impossibilities and impracticability in actual working. All hypothesis and theories put forth have a base of observation and comprehensive perception of the entire facts. All conclusions in this book have a base of enormous data and its analysis. Practical situation, theoretical analysis and relevant conclusions are based on the real case studies of various industrial spaces. Business Vaastu is a complicated subject because it involves many complexities related to energy streams, five great elements and planetary continuity.

Take an example, a factory followed every aspect related to traditional Vaastu strictly in its construction, processing and distribution. But within 6 months the factory started showing huge losses. In my case study and rigorous analysis it was found that huge containers with blue colour were culprits in energetic of Vaastu. The entire movement of such containers from east to north, north-to-northwest, and west in an anticlockwise direction created a Saturn Ring to positive energy zone. Blue colour represents Saturn element and when moved in an anticlockwise direction it effected a reversal of energy loop and helix. Many such factors are involved in guessing the helix of energy. A forward movement of helix of energy rotates the wheel of time leading to a forward rotation of wheel of Karma (= deeds). This helical streaming of energy effects the manifestation of fortunate events in the history of an industry. There are many books devoted on the subject of administration and management of events in commercial and industrial spaces. The beauty of this traditional Vaastu Shastra is that it speaks of creations of positive events and not of permutations and combinations of events. Rhythm, synchronicity and frequency are the main axes of this field of energy. Confluence points of these three dimensions are the nodes denoting progress, prosperity and peace.

2

SPACES: WOMBS OF CREATION

Frank Lloyd Right, a legend in the field of architecture quotes that "spaces are wombs of creations". A simple definition of the word space is "space = void+ energy". "Where there is space there is life, and where there is void, there is death." This equation of space is the principle of Vaastu Shastra. The entire concept and fact of event manifestation is related to this definition of space. In the traditional concept of Vaastu Shastra space is *Aakash*, energy is *Prana* and void is *Yama*. All ancient science use symbols as the carrier of comprehensive meaning. If symbol is understood properly, one gets the application of shastra. The concept of energy related to space is subtle and comprehensive. All the known sources of energy are like carrier signals of Prana. Generally this energy called Prana does not cross the limitations and constrains of spectrums of known energies. Since Prana is subtle, it has some unknown virtues, which sometimes make all these shastra as mystique sciences. In certain exceptional cases, one finds that energy called Prana is not following the above mentioned rules. In all such cases, certain other factors like five great elements or time plays an important role. Prana remains silent and choiceless cosmic existence creates such exceptions. Such incidents do not happen when the cosmic order and discipline is followed critically and strictly. In totality, on the comprehensive screen, the cosmic equations do not go wrong. In event manifestation, a path of least travel and friction is the route of time on which the entire matrix is dynamic along with changing vector of direction. It is a volatile alchemy with rules of a larger set and not of that set which exists. A new factor introduced becomes a leader to transcend the valley of negation in to a sky of freedom. This new factor is the vector, which Vaastu Shastra formulates as the angle of success and event. Entire Vaastu Shastra is the art of formulating such angles in the 3D matrix of time, directions and individual. Two spaces in equi-rhythm, nurture a good architecture where "self" gains the momentum of action, thought and speed. In Business Vaastu, this rhythm of spaces plays a very important role leading to a frictionless, blockage free, and impedenceless streaming of cosmic energy. A man is a cosmic miracle that tries to equalize the valley of disparity of Nature and tries to transcend the differences in various aspects of Nature. This study of Nature has given birth to the ancient shastra.

The great failure of Enron is a correct example of faulty soil and zone. The land of Dabhol has sea to south/southwest/west zone. Even to some southeast part nearer the project, there is a deep sea coast. Whenever the land slopes to the south, southwest and west zone, the pingala streams attack the entire zone, causing calamities which can lead to death, destruction, demolition, discontinuity and defamation. Probably these five bitter experiences were tested by a government body. At least, where huge investments are concerned, government should respect our traditional science by following some minimum constraints as explained in the theory.

3

Environmental Aspect

Since environmental constraint is a prime factor in architectural studies, variation in planning is obvious for different parts of world. All the factors related to environment are mostly dependent on the relative position of the sun. The Sun is the focus paint in aligning the various parts of houses, buildings and industrial shades. It is done in a way that northern, central and southern hemispheres are such located that earth and sun relation, angle of alignment, quality of solar rays, seasons, and requirement of human being has varying dimensions in day-to-day life. Along with these dimensions of the sun, earth as a matter of independent element plays an important role that has been rightly pursued in the Indian Vaastu Shastra. In modern architecture, solar path and temperature gradients are considered in the analysis but the role of earth along

> The business market and industries show some fantastic irregularities regarding growths and profits in some products, like some temporary comets in the sky. In a short duration the comet starts dissolving the aura and spread becomes a flashy soil. Often one can read such events through their symbols. The symbol of "Satyam" has a vertical cobra like ascend but has a dissipating void at the bottom representing a baseless growth.

with its hidden virtues is not taken care of. The role of earth and zones of earth are the main factors of analysis in Indian Vaastu Shastra. This part is a mystique and needs a careful approach to understand the underlying principle. Some minor differences in planning are necessary according to the variation in the environment. This environmental variation in planning is related to the physical phenomenal comfort, which is just a 10% part of shastra. The important aspect of shastra is related to the psychological, spiritual and organic content of the human being.

In European countries, Sun is a luxury. Temperature does not rise from more than 20'C. Solar radiation and its ill effect is not a focus point in architectural planning. Projecting the living spaces to the sun and protecting them from chilly gusty winds is the target in architectural planning. The sun acts like an element that provides warmth. Hence terraces to south and west, sloping roofs to south and west, are a common consideration in planning. Closing the north and opening the south creates warm living spaces. With respect to this environmental constraint in traditional Vaastu Shastra, such houses are called as "SUKHALAYA" (houses with happiness).

In tropical countries, sun is a main encroaching factor that disturbs the spaces by temperature and radiations, so in architectural planning creating shadows and keeping the sun away is the principle in planning. A temperature graph in tropical countries shows the figures with high difference. Even in a day's graph this variation reaches to 40' C — the gap of lowest temperature in a day and highest temperature rise in a day reaches to 40' C leading to high thermal torque in environment. Positioning and proportioning of windows is based on this factor of high solar radiations.

In European countries water element has a tendency to enter in the crystal form, i.e. snow. Crystals have divine relation with light. Aryans while travelling through

Himalayas defined water as light, nectar of life, ever flowing and expanding medium etc.

Water contains a flame, a nectar, life and Prana that leads to truth of existence. The goddess of wealth Laxmi has emerged from water. A right expression of the water element in living spaces has an immense effect on prosperity and peace. The water element is equated to the north zone. The entire USA and European zone falls in north hemisphere of the earth. In history, relative north zones have always ruled the southern parts due to this better virtuous expression of water element.

Unless the water element, these organic streams and *Jaivik urja*, is graced by *Pranik urja* (solar reference Aditya Pravah) it has no divine value. The mind is represented with the water element and the intellect is associated with the sun element. A positive confluence of Pranik and Jaivik, i.e. organic and solar or mind and intelligence is the prime purpose of Indian shastras.

A weak solar expression, reduced contribution of east direction and absence of Prana in general, has been creating problems related to east-west axis in the USA and European countries. Problems related to east-west axis are related to rhythm and synchronicity. The intellectual capacity that bridges the gap between body and mind is weak, leading to loneliness, distracted families, psychic diseases, vices like drinking drug addictions, etc. A fragmentation at body and mind levels leads to frustrations, insomnia, addictions and weak moral values. So in architectural planning and interior designing it is necessary to raise the "east virtue" by proper use of colours, crystals, lights, pyramid floorings, landscapes, plantations, etc.

In tropical countries the water element has a tendency to enter in vapour form. Hence the virtue of north is missing in the tropical environment. South acts like a fire with the existence of the scorching sun and high thermal radiation. Problems in tropical countries are related to the north-south axis. The north deficiencies lead to poverty. The south aggression leads to death, destructions, discontinuities, etc. Generally "east west axis" is quiet. Enhancement of water element to north and earth element to south is the key to unhindered planning in tropical countries leading to a good family life, cultural reference, god fearing minds, people with better intellectual capacities, etc. So while planning in tropical countries one needs to take care of the issues related to the north-south axis.

In examples like "Satyam" the basic shape of the building reflects deceit and a wrong culture. All such places have north-south length with lot of aggression of west represented by "C" shape. The deity of west is Varun (Harshal) and has vices like unpredictable behavior and false presentation that ultimately leads to disagreement in every walk of life.

4

EARTH ELEMENTAL ASPECT

The entire mass of universe is originally the content of the Sun. Qualities of this mass changed according to the distance, orbit and speed in due course of time. Basically all the matter is a uniform entity that has emerged out of sun. This basic truth is the principle of "earth elemental aspect". Contents of the earth contain all the virtues and qualities of the entire universe. Hence in the womb of mother earth, one finds all qualities of all planets. Rather earth contains the dormant seeds of all planets that are lying in relevance to the zones and directions. Since Vaastu Shastra is a two-stream theory with reference to stream one can define the pattern of these seeds. This is known as *Ghat-Bimb Siddhant*, that is "as in macrocosm, so in microcosm". Energy in the earth element can be classified on the basis of directions, two streams, five great elements and these seeds of planets. So in Vaastu Shastra this concept of contribution of planets in the "space in and space around" plays an important role. The entire success of the Vaastu is dependent on the right expression of these seeds of planets in and around the living spaces.

The virtues, classifications and qualities of planets are the theme of Astrology. The entire frame of logic in Vaastu Shastra is based on the school of Indian astrology, slopes and gradients of plot, colour and content of soil, position of water source, placement of structure on plot, alignment of building on plot, reference of solar path and positioning of five great elements in planning. These decide the contribution of the earth element in the Vaastu Shastra. Earth is such a powerful element that it can correct the deficiencies of energy axis. As explained earlier for European countries and the USA, east-west axis is weak and for tropical countries north-south axis is weak. The fundamental deficiency of zone can be bridged by right expression of the earth element. The effects of planets explained in astrology are derived out of various combinations of different planets. Vaastu can cure all these negativities by the right expression of the earth element in the construction of houses, factories, industries, etc. For example, astrologically Saturn represents contraction and sinking. In Vaastu, with reference to two-stream theory, west is the sink zone of solar energy and south is the sink zone of organic energy. So Saturn's qualities are already seeded in the relative south and west zones.

North represents the water element. Water is qualitatively closer to the characteristics of the moon. So the moon governs the north zones. East represents main source direction of Prana. Prana is qualitatively closer to the characteristics of the sun. So sun represents the east zone. The natural horoscope with Aries as the ascendant is the base to decide the zones and seeds of planets. Twelve signs, nine planets, five great elements, ten directions are interrelated. This interrelation ship is the base of concept of the earth element in Vaastu Shastra. Integration and

> Flashy fluorescent colours and neon signs create the voids, where Rahu rules. Rahu is the king of the present period as Rahu represents the polluted poisonous orbit of wind element. The mall culture in the present time is based on these fluorescent lights and neon signs, where a new negative revolution is breaking the divine orders of Jupiter, Venus and Moon. Even the good business and good products are also forced to follow these techniques for a better survival.

deterioration are the two ends of any process. In an ending there is a new beginning. This cyclic mode of nature is known as wheel of time. According to Zen Buddhism this wheel rotates on the central pivot support of "Self". "Self" is the expression of wheel of deeds. That's how wheel of time and wheel of deeds are interrelated. Since Time is the part of space, continuum any change in space rotates the time. Wheel of time unwinds the self. The "Self" identifies the wheel of deeds. This identification of self-relocates the universe. So spaces, directions and time play a virtuous role in the life of human beings.

In traditional Eastern philosophy, the existence is divided in three states, viz. Satva (divine), Rajas (mix) and Tamas (evil). These three states are governed by the three deities—God, Man and Ghost. These three elements abide to the entire existence. Man is the link that decides the quality of time as per his association with the divine or evil. Mankind is a gathering of these three levels, viz. physical phenomenal, psychological and spiritual. His becoming and his future is a reflection of his constitution. This constitution happens out of the contribution of surrounding Nature. Elements of his constitution are nothing but the reflection of his surroundings. Vaastu principles lead to a positive matrix of energy where mankind gets related to divinity, i.e. Satwa. Vaastu offers a choice to get related to light and end the darkness.

A cosmic body of Vaastu Purusha is divided in 81 squares. Around 45 deities rule these 81 squares. Rather if a construction of a house or factory is according to the Vaastu principle then these 45 deities emerge as aura and define the limits of the cosmic body of Vaastu Purusha. This cosmic body creates a power in the directions which can be termed as aspiration. The moment the zones and directions get the energy streams, a power of five great elements emerges in these zones. A right place of five great elements gives a unique impedance free and frictionless placement to the house in the universal existence. This dynamic state of balance can be called a state of natural frequency. It is a state of positive confluence of individual breath and universal breath. A balance of spin, rotation and a cyclic motion is called natural frequency. Any system that attains the natural frequency automatically becomes a part and a whole of natural order. The entire eastern philosophy has emerged from this mega principle of natural order and natural frequency. The modern science of 21st century, which speaks of free will, free choice and interconnectivity of all systems, can digest this organics of natural frequency. Scientist with Newtonian old order may find it difficult to understand this comprehensive thought of Eastern philosophy.

Why are Chitale in Pune, Hafeez Contractor in Mumbai and Norman Foster in London successful? As they have a correct form and right relationship to the light.  Excitation of north and reloading the south is the most popular slogan of Vaastu, if followed correctly then there are chances to become Chitale, Hafeez and Norman Foster. Chitale Sweet Mart has road to north and east with lunar shape to northeast. Travel of light is from north to south and east to west, i.e. from source to sink. Lunar shape to northeast means as a matter of form, water is to northeast. Northeast streaming leads to divinity and monopoly. Large number of people in Pune use sweets of Chitale as the *naivedya*, offering to their beloved deities.

5

ENERGY ELEMENTAL ASPECT

The oriental philosophy is based on symbols. Symbols speak of spectrums of energy, aura and existence. Sound vowels related to these symbols correlate the rhythm. This rhythmic coexistence creates a momentum in the cosmic body. This momentum is nothing but a Prana that governs the play of universe. One who understands this grammar of notes, symbols and rhythms can create an abode where mankind can live in peace and bliss. Vaastu Shastra is an art of correlating these notes, symbols, sounds and rhythms in a practical way to create a surrounding where mankind can think, live and act in a state of free choice and free will. Normally energy lies in three states. Whenever these three states are in dynamic balance the forth state emerges as the rhythm. In Eastern philosophy *Agni* (fire), *Aum* (primordial sound) and *Vani* (power of speech) are classified as the four-way expressions. Fire contains heat, smoke, flame and light. Aum contains A (beginning), U (organizing), M (ending) iim (flowering). Power of speech contains *Vaikhari* (speech by tongue), *Madhyama* (speech at a deeper level, say a thought), *Pashyanti* (speech at a still deeper level, say a self) and *Para* (speech at the deepest level, say a Universal consciousness). This Agni has created the power of speech well said in *Aitareya Upanishad*:

Agnirvag bhutva mukham pravishat...

In the human body and in the universe various expressions are like different forms of Agni (fire), in other words like different forms of energy. In a way, different deities in an 81-grid analysis of Vaastu are different forms of Agni (fire). This Agni (fire) gets its medium from peripheral deities like Hiranya, Suvrata, Laxmi, Vibhuti, etc.

These deities form the channels of Prana in the cosmic body of Vaastu Purusha. A combination of this Prana and Agni creates a *Mandalacar* streaming in the cosmic body of Vaastu Purusha. This Mandalacar expression of energy is the sole purpose of existence called as *Pranava (Aum)*.

Dnyaneshwar quotes as,

(Pranancha pranauchi karawa) ....

Transform the Prana in to *Pranav*, i.e. let the Prana stream in a mandalacar way. In a Vaastu Purusha, Mandala Shikhi, Aryama, Aaditi, Anal, etc. are different forms of Agni (fire). A right relationship with Agni (fire) leads to light. In Vaastu Gayatri it can be explained as, *Tat kalay vidmahe mahadishayai ch dhimahi tanno vaastuh – prachodayat*.

Understanding the time as the expression of direction will lead the house to light.

In modern language all this can be explained as follows.

The office of a popular architect in Mumbai is L-shaped that opens out to northeast zone. The southern limb of "L" is at higher level. (Satisfying the law of Vaastu as south=high and north=low). The western limb of the space is at lower level. This zone has double height, means northern air column is powerful and southern earth element is established. In traditional language this shape is called Dakshin Pashchim Dvishala. "One who operates through such a form, becomes a king or monopolist in the business." This prophecy of Shastra and Hafeez's esteem in the market are matching the practical events.

"Rhythmic vibrations lead to waves. Rhythmic waves create the synchronicity, i.e. sound. Rhythmic sound creates the natural frequency, i.e. light. A collective harmony of vibrations, waves, sound and light is the dynamic balance of the Nature, which is a sole purpose of Vaastu Shastra.

Whenever Prana travels in a mandalacar path, Chi creates spaces in the zones, this gives strength to the aspirations of different directions, this powerful aspiration contributes virtue in life. So when Prana becomes Pranava, spaces get a light and aspirations fulfil the life. Swastika represents a double helix. Swastika is a right symbol of the entire theory of Vaastu Shastra. Traditional Vaastu Shastra speaks of Swastika-Gram (a town planned on swastika as a basic form). Swastika as shown in the figure contains 4 letters surrounding the Aum. These four letters are primordial sound (para vaani) of the deity of that zone. Whenever the four zones are tuned to a particular frequency these primordial sounds create a vibration of Pranav (Aum) in the centre. This Pranav in the centre is a cosmic breath of deity "Brahma", which is called as Vaastu Brahma.

DEITY	ZONE	MANTRA
Nanda	SE	*Ham*
Bhadra	SW	*Sam*
Jaya	NW	*Sham*
Rikta	NE	*Shham*
Poorna	Central	*Aum*

A formation of a double helix through the streaming of energy leads to a right expression of five great elements.

In industrial structures this theory has a technical reference. Unless the entire process of a production, type of materials, volumes and weight of machines is understood, alignment and position of axis is analysed, application of above theory is not possible. Business Vaastu is a complex subject which contains the problems related to basic Vaastu and constraints related to processes involved in the industrial layout.

Vaastu has direct correlation to the biorhythm, hence to the body, mind and intellect of persons involved in that space. Analysis of pattern of work on the basis of nature of the person is dependent on the zones and planets. Different duties, works and processes are controlled by different planets and zones. Hence if zones do not match the activity, it will lead to some type of friction and impedance. After all destiny is attained through the mind. Mind is related to the inner and outer spaces. Spaces are vibrating energy enclaves. Vibration is a contribution of lights, shadows, loads, plants and landscapes, i.e. Vaastu.

Many times zones and persons, zones and duties, zones and processes may not match in the total constraint of the industrial layout. In such cases an independent qualitative analysis of that zone helps to solve the issue. A standard set of rules to improve the virtue of spaces, should be used and should be made applicable to each individual unit.

> One simple remedy to reduce the effect of sunstreams is to reload the south, southwest and west zone. Hence in the main cabin of the chairman keep 50 kg lead pyramid of golden colour to southwest zone, 35 kg lead pyramid of yellow colour to south zone and 15kg lead pyramid of blue/silver colour to west zone. This ratio-proportion of heavy lead metal will do the contraction of the Vikat, Putana and Jambuk the Vikshep deities of south, southwest and west. Just one remedy is enough to create a virtuous change in the cosmic energy.

Business Vaastu is a vast subject. Each industry has a unique process. Raw materials, pattern of machines, pattern of processes, requirement of power, type of finished product, involvement of various chemical, thermal mechanical and different energies, various actions, and type of clientele—all these dimensions are involved in the scope of industrial Vaastu. Each process, material, colour, action and type of energy is controlled by different planets. Accordingly these zones are classified. In practical industrial planning, it is not possible to follow these theoretical constraints. A balanced compromise to run the show is an art of Vaastu Shastra. Comprehensive understanding of all these factors leads to a practical solution. Definite sets of rules given in this book are based on study of failures of various industries and reflection of their conditions in traditional Vaastu-shastra. Case studies contain all the areas of India, e.g. Maharashtra, Gujarat, West Bengal, Goa, Karnataka, etc.

If in some factory, roof slopes are to south and west, then this disturbs the thermal equation, creating imbalance in the biomagnetism attached to it. Entire energetics of the factory gets disturbed. Multiple folds of anticlockwise loops of negative energy kill the main deities in the Vaastu purush mandal. This high thermal torque create panic in the aspirations and zones. In such cases a tremendous rise in the quantity and content of the earth element in south/southwest/west zone is absolutely essential to improve the condition of the factory. After this correction relocate the transparent sheets in the roof in the relative north and east zone, so that travel of light from source zone can stabilize the positive deities of the Vaastu Purush Mandal.

6

SUCCESS, FAILURE AND LIQUIDATION

Many times the product in the market is of good quality but due to improper marketing the product fails. Often the product in the market is of very good quality but the distribution system can abstain the spread of the product.

Frequently a small mistake in wrapping the product may create displeasure and denial from consumers. A product fails at times due to a religious or national sentimental spirit getting hurt or often due to a some small reaction after the use of the product that gets connected to the social health conditions. An ardent necessity of the product may command and overrule all other negative elements. Many times some political institution may create an obstruction for distribution of the product.

Creativity, productivity, marketability, aggressive advertising utility distribution system, a traditional grace, modern approach in techniques, least production cost, labour support, etc. are various factors that decide the success or failure of the product. All these factors fall under the control of various planets and their combination. So all these factors fall under the control of different aspirations of zones and directions. Unless a mandalacar streaming of energy happens in all spaces of the industry, the various aspirations may not contribute to the positivity. A deep thought is needed which includes these mystical elements, directions, zones, energy streams along with a practical flow of technical know-how. Like a reparatory in homeopathy or symptomology in allopathy, a coordinated study is necessary before planning a Vaastu.

Success and Nature both have a lot of hidden network of logic. A consistency in research, an open eye of observation, open mind with flexibility and high digestive capacity to absorb the poisons are the four pillars of success. Vaastu Shastra by connecting the broken loop of energy can create a situation, where all the four pillars above can get a solid foundation. When each direction is planned to suit its element, planetary positivity and its own nature as source and sink, automatically cosmic energy starts streaming in a mandalacar way leading to peace, prosperity and progress.

It is interesting to know about how the great industrial empires got ruined when basic rules of Vaastu Shastra were violated. On observation the fault is largely found in the selection of a *Bhoomi*, i.e. a plot. The failure of SM-Dyechem in Kurkumbh industrial estate, Enron in Dabhol, Garvare on Pune Satara Road are certain definite cases which have

> When the purpose of the form is entertainment, gambling, prostitution, financial transaction, immoral freedom, bars and all types of non-vegetarian foods then the excitation of west plays an important role. Varun and Jambuk deities are supportive to all the above characters. Normally all such spaces have its working hours and flooding of people after the sunset, when the power of west starts ruling the sky. Clubs, hotels and discotheques are counter places and alternatives to the 7th house in the horoscopes. Even structures like "C" opening to west, i.e. Varun-choola also gives a fantastic result for such purpose. Even activation of northwest also plays an important role in such activities.

violated the constraints related to the selection of plot, i.e. *Bhoomi-Nikash*. Specifically 90% industrial layout in Mahad industrial estate is locked due various reasons, where the plot itself represents a total negative energy field. Around 80 small-scale units in the Mahad industrial estate represent total failure.

In the places like Ichalkaranji and Nashik some spots have excellent geographic conditions, evidently showing success and progress.

Apart from all such natural ill sequence of elements, Vaastu Shastra has its powerful domains of remedies, which can create a well going happy condition. A particular form of building to suit the surrounding, a particular distribution of units of the factory to suit the planetary sequence and a particular pattern of processes to suit the energy axis, may form a key to success while planning for the industrial layout.

A Godrej industrial estate in Mumbai, Vikhroli, has shown a steady graph of success. Position of huge liquid containers to south zone and north-south axis of the buildings, is the key to success in this industrial area. (Figure 11.3)

Energy, matter, elements, aspirations and the form play important roles in the success of any structure. Either of the three constraints mentioned above should be positive for a minimum level of the appreciation of the space. In any industrial structure, it is easy to rectify the "energy – matter equations" by readjusting the light in the spaces and by creating artificial depressions in the surroundings. A grace of element can be carried in the space by using different shapes and colours. If proper thought is given, without majour changes in machinery layouts, one can artistically play to create the vibrant spaces.

A careful survey of successful units and a critical analysis of failures is the basis to learn Vaastu Shastra. In this book we will discuss all these aspects in detail through various case studies and will confirm them on the hardware of traditional Vaastu Shastra.

To produce goods and services is the main aim of all industrial estates. Natural resources, capital, management, labour and technology are five-fold inputs to run the industry. All these five activities and entities are under the control of different combinations of planets; hence their relationship with different zones is the key to Vaastu Shastra. Goods and services produced are called outputs. Natural resources can be classified according to planets, e.g. oil is equated to Saturn; red things are equated to mars; expanding materials are related to Jupiter. Hence classification of natural resources is based on many factors like colour, substance, quality, fluidity, solidity, density, smell, touch, form, etc. Management is the dimensions of Sun, Jupiter and Mercury. Some tinge of Mars also plays an important role. Advertising is the dimension of Mercury and Venus. Research and development are related to Jupiter, Harshal, Neptune and Mercury. Skilled labour represents a combination of Venus and Saturn; labour involved in hardship is a combination of Mars and Saturn; repetitive job is the activity of Saturn. Hence an industrial venture needs a careful approach while planning according to the Vaastu principles. It is a complex subject, which requires a thorough knowledge of zones, planets, five great elements and energy streaming. Often industrial processes, alignment of machines and ratio proportions of space are fixed then it is a real challenge for a Vaastu expert to blend the Vaastu principle and practical needs. Here, a deep knowledge of characters of directions is essential. Concerning, cosmic energy, there are different patterns of energy source. Each direction contributes some virtue to the space and total contribution of all directions formulates a totally new dimension to the existence. A harmony and cosmic balance is possible only by proper contribution of different directions in the total content of different energies. "A blending of opposite elements, directions and zones should lead to the helical streaming of energy" — this is the main difficult task for Vaastu experts.

Any individual, his aspirations and his activities unless tuned to the environment, cannot contribute his inner self, his excellence and his skill. That's why we say, "Vaastu acts like a bridge that connects inner and outer spaces that correlates self to the Nature and is the key to flower the divinity. Success and failure of any industry depends on many such factors. As mentioned earlier, largely it is a two-pronged process. One contains inputs and other contains output."

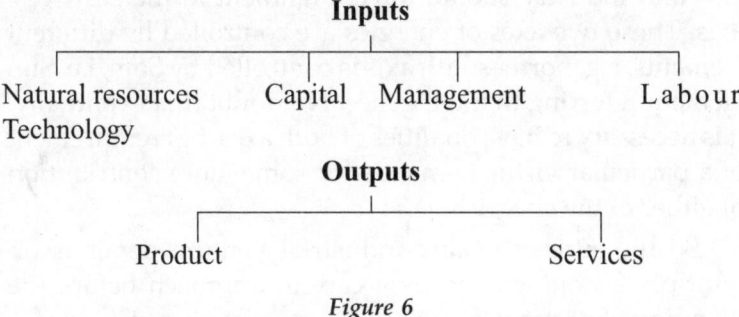

Figure 6

All these factors are interrelated and a collective forward working may lead to success.

For example: If a sugar industry was planned on the principle of Vaastu Shastra, but due to a drought it could not collect sugarcane. If a steel plant was based on the Vaastu principles, but due to government rules mining in that area becomes difficult.

All these possibilities are clubbed under one principle in Vaastu Shastra. It states that all sciences work in the limits of placement, time and surroundings, in traditional words we say, "*Sthal, Kaal and Sthithi*".

Ever changing nature of time, man, place and pattern should be considered as the most important factor while applying the system of all these divine sciences.

Business and industry are two pillars on which prosperity and progress of any society rests. Business is based on the cleverness and industry is based on the services. In a way both these pillars have some opposite elements but in totality they are complementary to each other. Their boundaries and oneness are vague and ever changing. Business and industry form a complex net and grid, where it is very difficult to analyse the role of each element as regards the success in totality. Overall, one can say that business should have alignment to the north-south axis and industry should have alignment to the east west axis. These two axes of energies are controlled by different elements, e.g. north-south axis is controlled by Som, i.e. Sun element referring to intelligence. No doubt that eventually, it is necessary to have qualities of both axes, but requirement of a particular virtue demands for some more contribution of either of the energy axis.

So the success of any industrial venture depends on multiple factors and needs a careful approach before the planning of a layout.

The subject has crossed the bounds and limits of basic nine planets. Moreover, it is in the zone of Harshal and Neptune, which are on the outer orbit of the Solar System. These planets have less affinity and lesser control of sun, but they carry the miracles of vast outer sky. The present market reflects the volatile characters, hidden virtues and unknown controls of Harshal and Neptune.

7

CLASSIFICATION OF INDUSTRIES

Classification of industries depends on various factors. Rather it is a most difficult task to analyse the pattern of industry. A detailed discussion with various authorities involved in the process and production, can classify the involvement of various factors, through which one can classify the industry, e.g. production of liquor involves organic chemistry, raw materials, temperature, boilers, colours, cooling systems and machinery. After production, the success is related to distribution, marketing, advertising, government rules, various departments and public response. So any production during the processing falls in the zones of various planets, and different five great elements. Many compromises and adjustments are necessary for the practical working of any system. This balancing of practical requirement and constraints is a real challenge for a Vaastu expert. How the problem of balancing this dimension is difficult can be seen through a simple example of a petrol pump.

Case study 1 - Petrol Pump

A petrol pump is an open structure where selection of land is based on the most important fact that the road has to be easily accessible. In case of petrol pumps, these are the problems.
   1. Entrance and exit to the property is from two corners of the plot which are along the main road. In all such

cases it is a Vaastu fault, as the main entrance and exit are preferred only through the 4th division of the front, which is the most auspicious sacred cut of the frontage.
2. If the petrol and diesel underground tanks are taken in the front zone of the property then the backyard of plot is at a higher level that leads to financial losses as per the Vaastu principles.
3. If the depression is in the north, northeast and east zones to accommodate the petrol and diesel, then as per the Vaastu rules it is a right slope and gradient to the plot. But the material stored being petrol and diesel, which represents Rahu and Saturn, does not suit the north, northeast and east zones.
4. Due to classification of material as Rahu and Saturn, this storage is suited to the south and west zones. Since this storage is possible only in the depression, i.e. underground tanks, this depression in south and west zone is a severe Vaastu fault.
5. Normally the required frontage of a petrol pump makes the plot of tiger face (Vyaghra-Mukh). This specific requirement for the easy circulation of vehicles again creates a severe Vaastu fault.

In a statistical survey carried out in last ten years, I have hardly come across a happy owner of a petrol pump. As a matter of principle of Ghat-Bimba-Siddhant, I have observed similar faults at the working places in the houses of these owners.

Through this small example one can understand that planning for a successful industrial layout needs a deep study of various factors involved in the process, production and principles.

Case study 2 - Zinc Ore Factory

Let us take a case study of a zinc ore industrial unit. An eminent Vaastu expert designs with this factory based completely on Vaastu principles. If the Vaastu expert does not have an astrological eye to analyse the planetary classification of process, product and raw material then it turns out to be a failure, irrespective of the fact that Vaastu principles have been followed. High temperature vessels of boilers are rightly placed in southeast zone. Material procurement is done from Northeast/east zones. Final product goes out from northwest zone.

During the process heaps of Zinc ore lies in north, south and southwest zones. Zinc represents Jupiter. Zinc is a sub-metal of Jupiter. Its cosmic properties represent all qualities of Jupiter that are expansion, light and source. Storage of this material in south and southwest zone gives a source character to these directions which is contradictory to their natural classification. Sun sets in the west, organic stream sets in the south so south, south west and west have a sink character, i.e. a Saturn character. Any material represented by Jupiter is not suitable for south, south west and west zones. A load equation of Vaastu may be right in this case but source and sink principle of Vaastu is not taken care of in this case. Many times quantitative analysis might be right but qualitative analysis disturbs the energetic of Vaastu.

Case study 3 - Middle East Countries

A Vaastu analysis of petrodollar

Middle East countries may lead to horrible future equations. At present for last 50 years they have enjoyed a very rich past, but the future may not be safe and healthy due to the removal of large quantities of oil from the womb of mother earth. Biomagnetism plays an important role in the process of eventology. Deeper excavations to negative zones disturb the energetics all around. Beginning of disturbance can be observed in the habits, symptoms and responses given by plants and animal kingdom. It is a type of break to the natural cycle of rhythm and existence, which has an all-round effect on total being and becoming.

Case study 4 - Steel Mill

Similarly a typical case of rolling steel mills is of different nature and classification. Iron ore is a combination of Saturn, Mars and *Pruthvi-Tatwa*. Scrap steel represents Saturn and Rahu. In feng shui even the form of material is also classified on the basis of five great elements. High level temperature more than 5000'C is used in the process. A stroke character of certain machines or shocks involved in mechanical processes represents the power of Mars, forms like rods and squares due to length are categorised as wood element.

Huge machines represent a big load and a heavy gravitation so are classified as Pruthvi-Tatwa. A cooling system involves water element and moon effects. Through such examples one can understand the complexity in designing industrial Vaastu.

Conclusion

Unless zones, directions, elements, materials and process are matched it is difficult to lead the industrial set up to success and stability. Axis of the process and geometric axis are two important axes while planning the industry.

When such a perfect situation is not possible, then by use of different elements, levels and mediums it is possible to clear the path of progress and creativity. This art of cleansing the energy stream and creating a positive field of cosmic energy is the main job of a Vaastu expert. In traditional shastra this effect of plants, auspicious stones and metals is called as "Prabhav", or "Aura". In short, light and aura are the powerful media which can control the activities of time. The sole purpose of shastra is to create a positive relation with light, so the Rishi says *Dhiyo Yona Prachodayat*.

8

MATRIX OF SPACE, TIME AND EVENTS

As said in *Bhagvad* Geeta, "every system has a beginning and end simultaneously, instantaneously and permanently." Eastern philosophy has found the truth of life as a pattern of cyclic expression. Definition of energy source is expressed as "Mandalacar", i.e. helical. It is a formation of three helical streams through which the fourth dimension of existence, i.e. life.

In Dnyaneshvari it is nicely expressed as "मात्रा त्रय मावळे ॥ अर्धबिंबी"

Life as a matter and energy, a combination of apparent and real is the basic expression of three streams of energy; of which the half source is visible and a half source is assumable. This assumable part is part of eternal existence and visible half part is part of changing existence. When these three streams of energy create a mandalacar pattern of expression, life emerges as bliss. Then it has a direct relation with the assumable half part of eternal existence. Then the time and directions are not bound and limited but they support the existence by a formation of a frame. In such cases the ending of a system becomes a transformation of a system leading to growth and bliss as the main factors of activity.

An alert Vaastu expert has one eye of observation on direction and one eye of vigilance on time; directions are related to streams of energy, whereas the time is related to eventology. Direction as a matter of dimension is a prime factor in Vaastu whereas time as a matter of dimension is the prime factor of Astrology. Their interconnectivity, interdependence and integral expression is the base of Astro-Vaastu. Only Vaastu has a static role; only Astrology has a limited role of dynamic powerful virtue to bend the curvature of time and to bliss the aspirations of Directions.

Sky as a whole is governed by the position of planets. The position of planets is decided in correlation to the series of constellations. A wave of energy that expresses an effective cycle of events in the cosmos can be read in correlation to these planets. Counter elements created in the living spaces has profound role to play by simulating cosmic planetary energy in correlation to five great elements in the house. Rather Vaastu principles act as the antidote on negative energy of planets, and simultaneously provide a frictionless path to positive energy.

With this understanding when we study the history of any Vaastu, then it is evident that why certain Vaastu gives negative result in a cyclic periodic pattern. Every Vaastu has a self-potential that keeps it in good condition and good health with the travel of time; a wave of negative energy starts its attacks on the boundaries of Vaastu. If boundaries of Vaastu are nicely sealed then these waves of cosmic energy slowly damp down and the Vaastu survives in the negative period. If the faulty zone of Vaastu and the direction of attacking cosmic energy match in the matrix of time, then the deterioration of Vaastu gets accelerated then the failure of Vaastu is definite and certain. Hence simulation of hitting waves of cosmic energy is the main purpose of Vaastu Shastra. Planning of Vaastu has immense importance, so that in the confluence of negative planets and in the combination of negative elements a strong inbuilt format survives and protects the people residing, accelerates the positive process and deletes the negative elements.

> All the religions mention of negative energy and events related to black magic. In the context of Vaastu Shastra to protect the self and the spaces of our office/house/factory, various remedies are given, which can be explained in the classical language as *Kavach* (shield) *Argala* (propagation of energy) and *Keelak* (nailing the negative spirits). The activity of Kavach is related to the deity Brahma. The activity of Argala is related to the deity Vishnu and the activity of Keelaka is related to the deity Shiva. All these rituals when performed in the Vaastu they create the vibration and rhythm of A-U-M, i.e. pranava or helical streaming or mandalacar form of energy. Well said by Saint Dnyaneshwara, i.e. transform the energy to travel in a mandalacar way: this happens when Vaastu undergoes the rituals related to Kavach, Argala and Keelaka.

Event is a confluence or clash of different elements, for e.g. fire is a combination of Agni, Vaayu and Earth. Where there is a confluence of elements one can categorise it as a process, whereas a clash of elements leads to the break in a process, which can be an accident, an explosion or a blockage. Time is counted on the various combinations of planets in the sky, in a way can be said as a super dynamic factor. A combination of positive elements creates a space whereas a combination of negative elements explodes the space leading to multiple voids. Art of Vaastu planning is an art of planning the processes, uniting the elements and observing the planetary effects. In feng shui every year a format of treatment varies. Whereas Vaastu is a designed vessel that automatically survives in highs and lows of cosmic energy. With time, a power gets generated in Vaastu that takes care of the dynamic time. One has to be alert in feng shui to take care of the dynamic time. Vaastu works on the cosmic body of the house whereas feng shui works on the format of the Nature, which is ever changing. In traditional language it is called as the three levels of existence and process, for e.g. *Anga* means body, *Aawaran* means cover and *Vikshep* means outer influence. In Vaastu Purusha Mandal, it is explained on the classifications of deities and zones. In feng shui it is explained on the characters of five great elements and subsidiary eight elements.

9

IDEAL INDUSTRIAL PLANNING

Ideal planning is a dream in golden night. What one can execute is a total balance of various factors by natural and artificial means. In a way ideal industrial planning is an art that removes the blockages, accelerates the mandalacar streaming, provide the uniform chi to all aspirations and flowers the bliss. Ideal planning requires conceptual clarity of the following factors.

a. **Two-stream Theory:-** North to south is the passage of organic cosmic streams. East to west is the passage of pranik cosmic streams. A positive confluence of these two streams is the purpose of Vaastu Shastra. Many times in living spaces, only one stream is available. In such cases by artificial means, indirectly the other stream is forced in the space to create the positive confluence of the two. This artificial forced cosmic stream is created through the space proportions, level difference, load adjustment and powerful ventilations.

b. **Five Great Elements:-** Many times, the industrial process includes the thermal sensitivity, chemical intensity, mechanical vibrations and variations in loads. In this classification, conflicting elements are involved in the same space, which may create chaos in balancing the cosmic energy. In such cases this effective balance is attained through right shape, colour, form and metal. A correct knowledge of astrology regarding the right expression of five great elements is necessary. For example, ice, water and steam are three forms of Hydrogen oxide, where ice is classified as Pruthvi-Tatwa with *jal*-virtue. Water is classified *Jal–Tatwa* with streaming virtue. Steam is classified as *Agni-Tatwa* with exploding quality and Vaayu-virtue. For industrial process, termination from one phase to the other creates the turbulence in Vaastu. Here the right understanding of elements and their virtues is essential to the Vaastu planners.

c. **Planetary identification:-** Each process has various stages. In each stage it passes through various forms of energy and matter. Accordingly during the process effect of planets keeps changing. Even as per the pattern of process the classification of planets keeps changing. For example,

1. Cutting to small pieces could be represented by *Ketu*.
2. Contraction leading to cooling could be identified with Saturn.
3. Explosion leading to high temperature could be Sun and Mars combination.
4. Explosion leading to poisonous gases may be attached to *Rahu*.
5. Exothermic process with expansion may be classified for Jupiter and Mars.
6. Endothermic process with expansion could be related to *Harshal* and Neptune.

Hence part taken by planets and process promoted by planets could be two aspects to analyze the planetary identification. Even colours can play havoc in creativity and productivity, if they are not used properly.

> If in some factory, the load of machinery lies in the north zone and comparatively south is empty then, a) Create depressions to the north-northeast zones of plots. b) Provide transparent sheets in the roof to the north zone. c) Reload the empty south zone by stones to raise the plinth level. d) Paint the south zone of roof using yellow/brown/black colour. e) Limit the light and ventilation from south zone. f) Provide towering pyramidal roofs to the south zones. g) Provide boreholes to north/northeast zones wherever possible.

   d) **Forms, Weights and Loads:-** A deep direct thought is given to "forms" in the form school of feng shui, wherein elements are equated to forms. In Vaastu, the analysis being based on two-stream theory, the forms have more finite meaning. Pyramidal forms represent four actions — "It holds, curtails, contracts and burns." So they create blockage to the streaming. So pyramidal forms should be arranged to the south, southwest and west zones, i.e. to the synk zones. Glossy, reflecting surfaces create accelerations to the light energy, so should be supplemented to the north and east zones. Brown, black, yellow colours with pyramidal forms and loads are excellent to absorb the negative currents of south zone. Objects or shapes similar to the stream line, i.e. fish shapes with reflecting silver surface are good for north, northwest and east zones.

   Towering forms and chimneys should not be placed to northwest, north, northeast and east zones as they create vortex and blockage in the cosmic streams.

   e) **Roofing Patterns:-** Roof is the most important factor as it acts like a diaphragm that connects the inner spaces of factories and outer vast sky. A curvature or angle given to the roof has great reference to the projection of unit to solar rays. Even befitting of shape in correlation to the eight directions adds virtues of sky in the central zone of Vaastu. In Vaastu Purusha Mandal deities in the inner wheel, for e.g., Vivswan and central Brahma *Mitra, Pruthvidhar, Aryama* get right excitation, if the roof has some symmetry and sacred geometry that binds the aspirations of eight directions. This sacred geometry of roof can force the cosmic energy to travel in a mandalacar way, so that deities in the four corners get a cosmic breath that flourishes the aspirations. Roof limits the infinite sky in to finite spaces where event can nurture. Roof propagates the light energy in a forward way where voids are deleted and spaces start rhythmic breathing. North light has immense meaning even in Western architecture where light enters the inner spaces from roof of north side. As already mentioned elsewhere, north is a source direction of organic jaivik streams, whenever light, i.e. pranik streams travel from north to south, these streams reinforce the quality of organic streams. This is a positive confluence of pranik and organic streams. In the process of event manifestation, this confluence has prime importance. Virtue and quality, order and discipline are different dimensions. Vaastu Shastra prefers to create the virtue and order through the understanding of nature. Traditional Vaastu Shastra gives more pressure on concept of Brahmsthan and Naabhi. This is the space where earth meets sky, yin meets yang. A "Bruhad-chakra", a comprehensive cycle gets completed by this cosmic meet. A seed of light "Ruby" which represents Sun- energy is placed at Naabhi-Node and at Brahmsthan. The light from north or from central zone excites the virtue of this Ruby. In feng shui this is termed as *Tai-Chi*. In Vaastu Shastra this is termed as *Tat-Sat* as explained elsewhere, since feng shui is a "No-stream theory" and Vaastu Shastra is a "two-stream theory"; the "Tai-Chi" represents single helix and Tat-Sat represents double helix.

The eye of yin in the body of yang or eye of yang in the body of yin is basically a *Mantrabeej*, a seed that creates vibrations, i.e. a seed that creates existence. It is the style of representing Mantrabeej by *bindu*, a dot in Indian Mantra

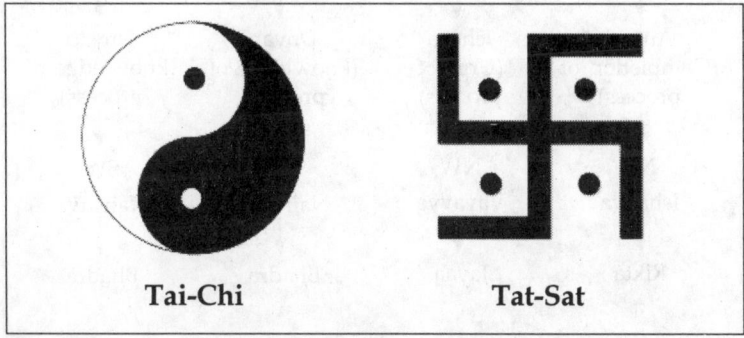

Figure 9

shastra, which is adopted by feng shui in Tai-Chi. In "Shreechakra" or in all Indian Yantras, this sequence and trio of *Naad,Bindu* and *Kala* is popular. Naad is vibration and rhythms. Bindu is representation and existence. Kala is expansion and progress.

All yantras are curvilinear, elliptical, and helical. Mandalacar represents progression of energy. Rather all yantras are forms and formulae through which one can get the path to propagate the cycles of cosmic energy. In traditional Mantra-Shastra, excitation of energy has four dimensions. All the dimensions are independent in existence and simultaneously exist in each other's womb; as if excitation of them depends on each other.

Energy cycle starts with rhythm, i.e. *Naad*. This rhythm due to its order leads to synchronicity, i.e. Bindu or *beej* or existence. This existence gets formulated in the deity, i.e. *Sakshat Devta* or experience.

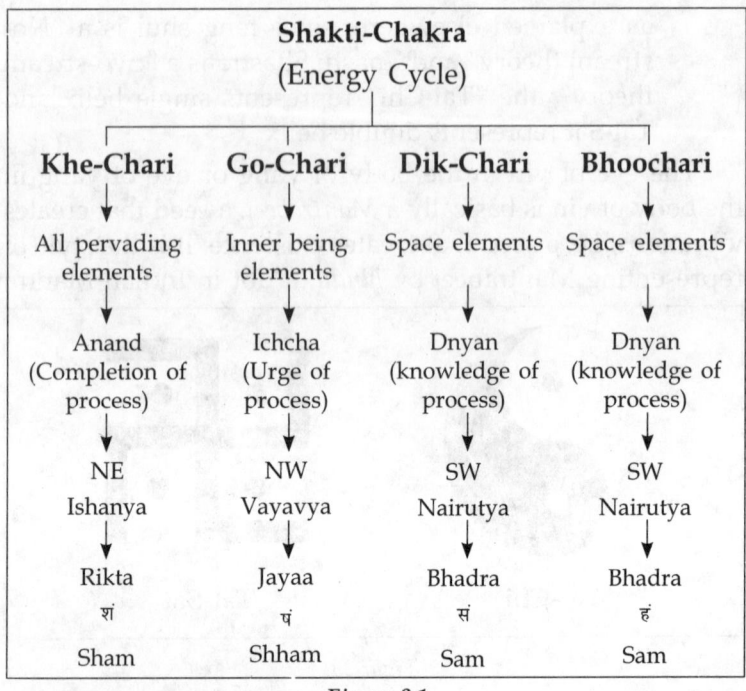

Figure 9.1

The Vedic definition says,

देवता या: तु शरीरं बीजात् उपपद्यते॥

Seed of vibration and rhythm gives the birth to the body of Deity.

Whenever earth and space element, i.e. yin and yang element, unite together in order the inner being gets tuned to the nature. This tuning of inner being expands "that" in to "thee", i.e. "Tat-Sat". In this condition, prana vibrates in the rhythm of Jal-Tatwa. In space prana and jeeva go in the cosmic union, this is a feng shui, i.e. this is a pawan-jal or a Vishnu-padodakam.

Excitation of various cosmic energy cycles is possible at ease, whenever the proper shape and size of roof touch the inner spaces of the house/factory and commercial premises.

f) **Ratio proportion:-** Proper high lows, length width proportions, its correlation to the heights, requirement as per the practical need and placements are of great importance in the mandalacar streaming of the energy. In traditional Vaastu Shastra more focus is given even to the body proportions of the owner of the house. The shapes and sizes of doors and windows are designed to suit the cosmic aura of the owner by considering the swami-hasta-praman (arm length of owner) as the basic unit of design. Normally as it leads to designs based on golden ratio, are considered as the sacred helical loops of energy in the travel of energy streaming.

In 9x9 or 10x10 division analysis of Vaastu, energy nodes represent the bindu- points. Whenever mandalacar cosmic breath touches these points "Bindu", they start breathing leading to a *Naad*. This Naad creates the expressions of an aspiration called traditionally as *Kala* or Aawishkar. Nand-Bindu-Kala, i.e. vibration-existence-expression completes the one circle helix of energy.

This gives birth to the seed or Beej, where there is this seed there lies the bliss of deity.

One circle, one helix, one event, one forward expression happens when process of Vaastu reaches this state of existence through a dynamic grid analysis.

Economy and financial constraints of one nation dictate the market and index of all the nations. One nation's economy depends on weapons and wars. One nation's economy falls due to hyper luxury and irresponsible expensive behavior of citizens in that nation leading to collapse of many financial institutes. This creates the thirst, hunger and droughts in many other nations. All these events reflect the violence of Rahu, terminating behavior of Harshal, mass suicide of Neptune and death of many comets.

In modern science all this is explained as rhythm, synchronicity and frequency as the basic terminologies related to the energy. This process of grid analysis is like tuning a musical instrument with vibration of Sa- "shadja" for a classical concert.

Energy division of this grid represents a specific deity and aura. It has a definite classification as regards the five great elements. It has a clear co-relation to the specific planet. Whenever this complete relationship exists, then such Vaastu acts like a mini-universe in the world of mega universe with least friction, less blockage and no impendence. Then such Vaastu acts like a cosmic yantra similar to Shri-Yantra, Bhairava-Yantra or Yogini- Yantra leading to peace, prosperity and bliss.

g) **Planning the gates, entrances and doors:** Doors act like a bridge that connects the inner spaces to the outer spaces. If a correct division is selected then outer system of nature becomes a friend of all the inner systems. An automatic positive play of power and cosmic energy begins. Doors act as a cut in a perimeter of a Vaastu. If this cut and the sacred cut in perimeter match each other then a positive process begin at the entrance itself. A traditional Vaastu Shastra is a two-stream theory. The central zone of directions acts as a passage of one energy stream, whereas the zone of sub-directions acts as the confluence of both streams. So any disturbance in the sub-directions creates a disturbance in both streams. On the contrary any disturbance in the central zone creates effect only on one stream. So doors, which act as a cut in perimeter, are never allowed in the zones of sub-direction. As a matter of cosmic truth for any direction, left represents moon-streams and right represents sun-streams. Doors act as passage of free energy streaming. So doors in traditional Vaastu Shastra are allowed in relative left zone of central part of that direction.

> In Mahad industrial estate, 50 km away from Mumbai, there are around 100 small-scale industrial units, out of which 75 units are closed. A huge investment is wasted due to non-functioning. The machinery worth crores of rupees is getting rusted for the last many years. This total zone has mountain range to north/northeast/east and the nalla, i.e. water zone is to south/southwest/west. Such situation means imbalance of "energy matter equation", loss of power of five great elements, multiple anticlockwise loops of negative energy creating malefic situation. Vaastu Shastra as an Indian style of architecture has given wonderful cosmic laws to select the land. If due respect is given huge financial losses can be avoided.

The path that leads from plot to house should be clockwise, i.e. *Pradakshinakar*. Hence

1. Where entry to the plot is from east, entry to the house is selected from south zone.
2. When entry to the plot is from south zone, then entry to the house/factory is selected from west.
3. When entry to the plot is from west zone then entry to the house is selected from north.
4. When entry to the plot is from north then entry to the house/factory is selected from east zone.

In traditional Vaastu Shastra these pairs of entries which form a clockwise path, i.e. *Pradakshina marg* is called as *poorna-bahoo-pravesh*. So if nine parts of any side of a plot are done then fourth division from left is considered as the auspicious division for door. As a magic of extension to the astrology this fourth division represents a moon sector. Moon acts as a mind that co-relates the outer and inner spaces in human being. One should take additional care while planning doors as follows.

1. There should not be a direct hitting road in this sacred cut fourth division of the side.
2. No tree or bund or stream should form a hurdle to the passage of energy.
3. Severe intense gradient and slop or a hillock is not a good sign in this zone.
4. Temple/mosque/religious place / church should not cast a shadow in the zone.
5. Huge pyramidal caps to the ceiling of watchman's cabin are not good to north and east entries.
6. Gates with automatic sensor arrangements are specifically denied in traditional Vaastu Shastra.

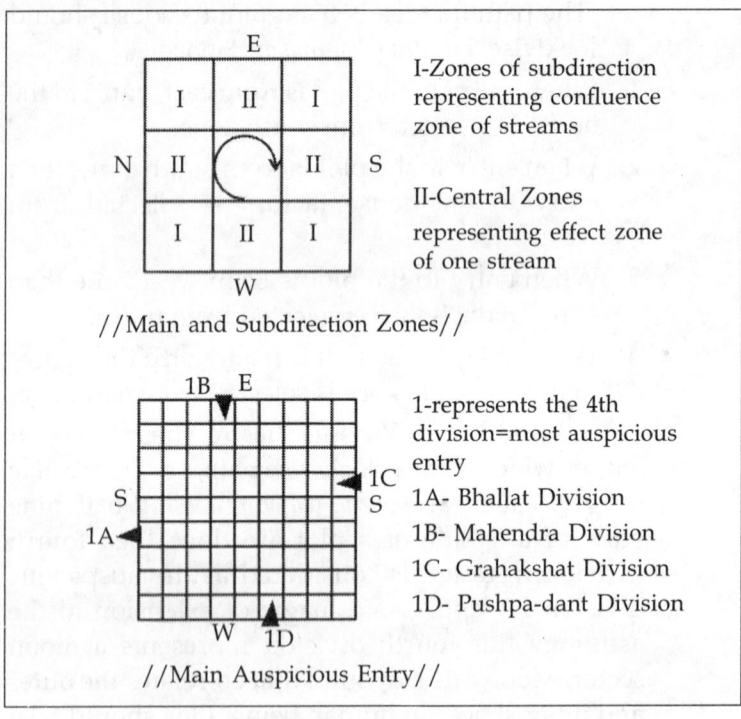

Figure 9.2

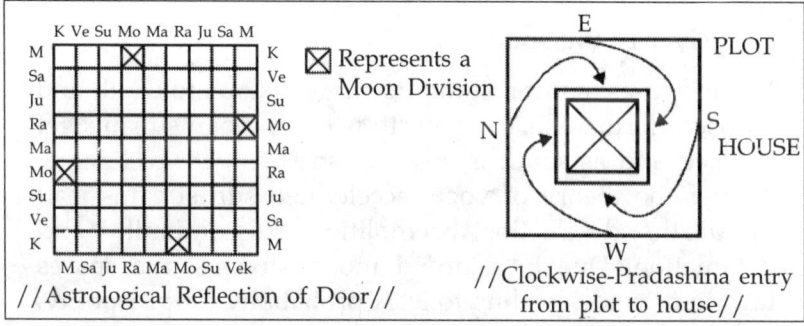

Figure. 9.3

h) **Natural site selection:-** In traditional Vaastu Shastra, highest importance is given to the "Bhoomi-Nikash", i.e. character of the plot. If the plot has mahadosh as regards the Vaastu- tenets, then all other constraints of theoretical Vaastu planning go to waste. Rather it is difficult to create a positive environment when basically nature does not support the planning. There are many practical case studies where this failure of industrial endeavour can be seen due to wrong characters of the plot. Following some fixed constraints and case studies are sufficient to understand the cosmic power of Vaastu Shastra.

Security safety and sensitivity are the main problems of modern world. Voids, violence and vulgarity are the important issues in front of everybody. Rhythm synchronicity and frequency is the only answer to all above problems and issues. The map of world and balance of earth is totally disturbed. Due to the drift of land, north is loaded by the earth element. South is getting excited by majority of water element. Axis of the earth is falling every 1000 years. This has changed the seasons, thermal constitution and global warming. In such a situation only Indian style of architecture speaks of mystique relation of nature and mankind through different deities, energy forms and SUN. To reduce the criminal behavior this branch of Vedic wisdom speaks on forms, elements, directions and aspiration.

1) River to the south:-

In such cases, natural contours show a slope to south and a raised north zone, since north is high, moon streams get blocked and as south is low sun streams get accelerated. As per the theory of yoga, accelerated sun streams lead to death, destruction, demolition, discontinuity and defamation. Due to retarded moon streams, the spaces turn in to voids, leading to least probability for prosperity, stability, peace and bliss. According to feng shui principles, water in backside zone wipes out the fame and prosperity. In feng shui south is equated to fire, so river in south zone reduces the power of fire element.

In my case studies I found following examples as examples of failure and defect. A big industrial set up of Garware nylon faced a fatal situation on Pune-Satara road where river flows east to west in south side of the factory layout. This major failure had some additional faults in the construction pattern of roofing and zone of the building.

Whereas raised huge water tanks to south zone in Godrej industrial estate in Vikroli, in Mumbai have created

---

No other system of architecture in the world has explicitly spoken on vibration, waves, sound and light with its organic relationship with the human life. How to subtract the noise and how to create the sound that gives positive energy is the basic theme in Vaastu Shastra by creating right proportions, sacred cuts and placement of elements in right zones. The right relationship to light leads to enlightenment and biorhythm which is the core of all the discussions of the oriental philosophy. The foundation of Vaastu Shastra is Vaastu Purush Mandal that speaks of different deities, which are different stages of sun, i.e. "light source".

a successful industrial estate. Due to a huge load of water and raised tanks of water in south zone, sun streams are retarded and get absorbed in the huge load. In traditional Vaastu Shastra it is called Urdhwa-Gurutwa.

2) Hills and Mountains to north and east zone:

This leads to the situation were ground slopes to south and west. As explained above, due to Urdhwa-Gurutwa to north and east, these directions and Moon streams get blocked.

North and east are source directions of organic and pranik energy. Due to hills and mountains in this zone, both natural energies get blocked. This situation transforms the space into voids. South and west are sink directions of organic and pranik energy. Due to high acceleration and slopes to south and west zones, negative energy enters these voids leading to evil black holes and vortex in the environment. Where there are voids and evil black holes, their life never nurtures and blooms.

> The treatment Kavach, i.e. shield is a ritual called "Vaastu nabhi". In the southwest zone of the central Brahma part of the plot, this ritual is performed, along with the southeast-column as the first auspicious act on the plot. Southeast-column is called "Agneya Sthambh". In this ritual on a good time (muhurth) a 6' x 6' x 6' pit is refilled with a Shanku at the centre by using river bolders. This high density zone in the Brahma, forces the energy to travel in a mandalacar way. Since this nabhi-node is eccentric and non-symmetric on the plot, with this node as the dynamic centre, or as the pivot point, the streaming of energy begins. This node classifies 5 divisions to water element and 4 divisions to all other elements, in a way gives more importance to water element which supports the streaming.

Out of 80 industrial units in Mahad industrial estate, 60 units are closed, due to bankruptcy or liquidation, as the Bhoomi- Nikash quality of plot is wrong. Entire north, northeast and east side is blocked by L-type range of hills and mountains. This situation has created the slopes to south and west. Water streams with flow towards south and west create negative energy in the atmosphere. West slopes give disagreement in every walk of life. Kurkumbh industrial estate on Pune-Solapur road has shown many failures due to similar natural situations of the plot.

3) **Sea Coast and Sinking Waters to SE, S, and SW Zones:**

Such a geographic condition is worst, as southeast representing fire and power, south representing main sink direction and southwest representing earth and stability are drowned in water element. Due to coastal areas being aligned to the plot, there happens to be a gradient and slope to that direction. Irrespective of who owns and who

---

Yog Vasishth, which is one of the oldest text on spiritualism, has defined "Vaastu Tatva" as सत्ता सामान्यम् अखिलम् वास्तुतत्त्वमिहोचते Here the first word "Satta" means the order of nature. "Samanyam" means "that merges with the fact" and reality, "Akhilam" means that which is "omnipotent". That which contains all these three dimensions, there exists the Vaastu element. This means all that reflects the order of nature and merges with the nature and exists irrespective of all odds is said as the Vaastu. Hence in the home, factory or office, so far as the container, contents and coordination match the time and direction, they will reflect the positive energy and progressive momentum.

supports the project, such a situation always leads to failure and defamation. In India a known example of such a failure is ENRON. Though it was a company owned by the mother-in-law of the president of US, nothing positive happened in the progress of the project. Afterwards it was supported by the Government of India and Maharashtra both, but still this could not work out till this date. The political people involved have taken away the cream and looted the public; again the artificial need to continue the project has been set up by government machinery. From the very beginning this project faced all kinds of disturbances. More than the fact that it was not Vaastu compliant, it seemed that god too was never keen on the success of the project. Tough days are continuing as the project faces a similar situation by cases in court, defamation and legal-social element.

i) **Energy, Axis and Form:**

In case, if site selection is not possible and there is no choice for alternative land, then one should follow these principles below in planning along with all standard tenets of Vaastu Shastra.

1. Observe that every building, shed and layout has a north-south length. This criterion has a great cosmic power which digests any poison and fault in Vaastu. Due to north-south length least perimeter gets projected to scorching sun. This leads to good thermal balance, leading to a better cool place and uniform bio-magnetism in and out of the project.

In the north-south length structures organic moon stream pass through the space for a longer time interval due to prolonged path. Whereas, in east-west length structures, moon stream pass through the space for a short five interval due to short path.

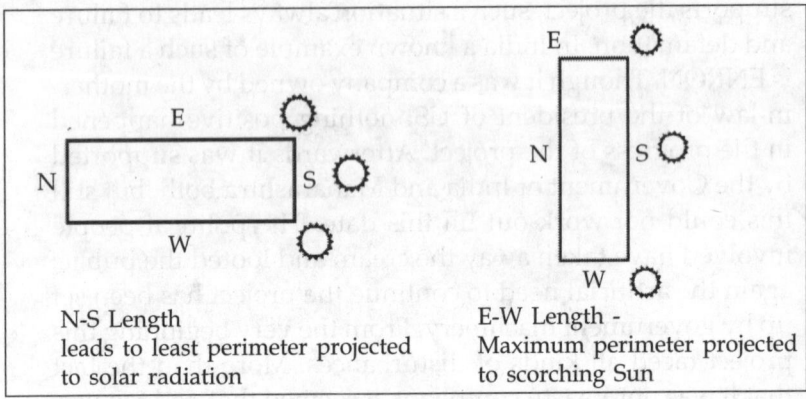

Figure 9.4

Moon streams represent bliss, stability, prosperity and bliss. Since in north–south length moon streams pass through the space for a longer time interval, they create positive energy fields.

All different styles of architecture have taken account of the climate, environment, use of local materials, solar path, etc., but nobody except Vaastu Shastra, i.e. Indian style of architecture, has taken keen interest to know the relation of time and directions, the house and eventology of the life, dynamics of cosmic forces and mandalacar - helical streaming of energy. Mysticism of nature and its connectivity to different forms of energy are very nicely dealt in this subject through different deities and their correct placement, alignment and sensitivity. No other system of architecture has taken the role of earth and its contribution in the human life except the Vaastu Shastra. Rather Vaastu Shastra is considered as the science that creates right expressions of all the five great elements.

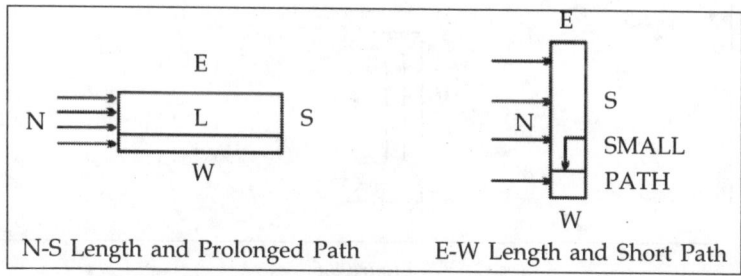

Figure 9.5

2. If the slope of ground is to the west then to reinforce the virtue of pranik axis construct the building with C-opening to east, i.e. *Poorva-Choola* constructions.

Since this form opening to east forces pranik energy to travel in a mandalacar path, such forms add virtue and order to the spaces and curtail the disagreement of west slopes. In Vaastu Purusha Mandal central east deity is *Aditya* that represents intelligence and prosperity. In this C-form the whole structure gets aligned around this powerful divine deity called as Aditya. Such C-forms opening to east get one more feature that "its main arm has north–south length."

One yellow-coloured pyramid in lead metal to south and one golden-coloured lead pyramid to southwest zone is a magic remedy to equalise the energy matter equation of the Vaastu. A solid stable earth element emerges in the south and southwest zone due to these pyramids, so that moon streams from north/northeast zone get accelerated power to reach south/southwest zone, through a helical path. Yellow colour represents the stability of the earth element, whereas golden colour represents the yang, prosperous, generative component of the earth element. So by colour, shape, metal and pyramid as the medium, a virtuous and qualitative earth element emerges in the proper zone.

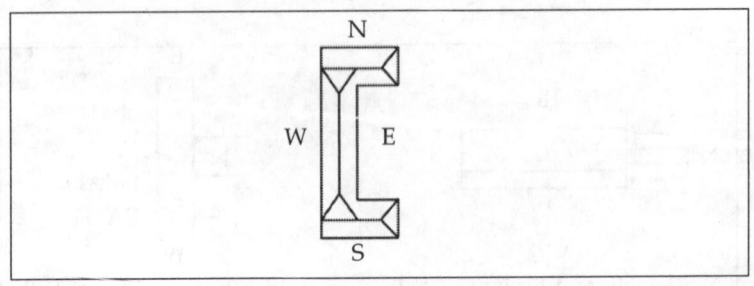

Figure 9.6

3. If the slope of the ground is to south then adopt the slope of buildings with "C-opening to north", i.e. *Uttar-Choola*-construction. Since this form opening to north, forces the organic energy to travel in the mandalacar way, such forms delete the effect of south slopes to some extent.

Given that in this form all deities of north join the deities in the central zone, cosmic energy of organic streams increases in a fantastic proportion. North represents Sun and Kuber and north represents water element. Hence these forms enhance the streaming of cosmic energy in Vaastu.

All the architectural colleges and syllabus contain studies of Islamic architecture, Gothic architectures or Roman style. It is unfortunate to know that there is no space for such a wonderful subject in the universities and colleges. This subject is so comprehensive, in nature that it covers the environmental aspect, use of local materials, cosmic comprehensive laws of nature, connectivity of man and nature, etc. This science through its parameters creates the energy continuum and protective shield so that the personal and cosmic breath are tuned to attain positive energy. Multiple dimensions of this science propagate a positive energy, which leads to positive events in life.

j) **Magnetic Asymmetry:**

If the plot is asymmetric as regards the geometric and magnetic axis then the problem differs in two ways.

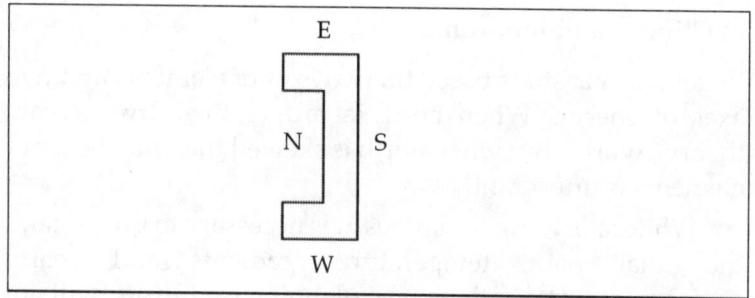

Figure 9.7

In type I northeast and southwest are longer sides whereas in type II southeast and northwest are longer sides. Comparatively the enhancement of water and earth element in type I is a better alternative than enhanced fire and wind elements in type II. Type II always leads to a great misery,

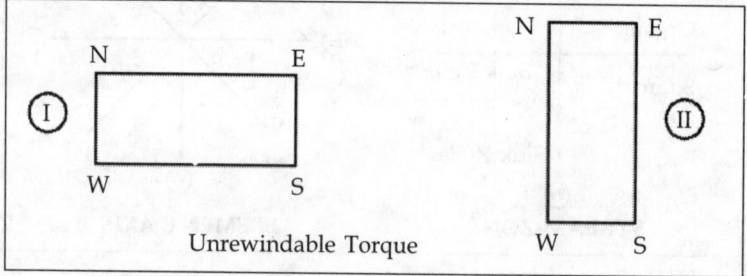

Figure 9.8

due to unrewindable torque of fire and wind at much closed domain. It is always better to divide the plot into both for type II so that the ratio of fire-wind axis with water-earth axis improves. In both cases it is advisable to take deep depressions to north zone to enhance the scope of organic stream. Rather if the entire north and northeast zone is provided with water bodies, borewells and depression then that will improve the quality of cosmic energy. Excessive towering minarets, platforms, and chimneys to south and west zone will reduce the possibility of vortex and explosion of cosmic energy.

k) **Climate and Environment:**

In general Vaastu is based on two axes of elements and two axes of energy. When north is proper then "two-stream theory" works. But when north is skewed then the theory of elements is important.

While analyzing the spaces, it is necessary to understand the solar path, temperature gradients and yearly environmental variations. The planning for Europe will not be suitable for Asiatic countries, e.g. north light roofs which are popular in Europe as sunlight is not very adequate,

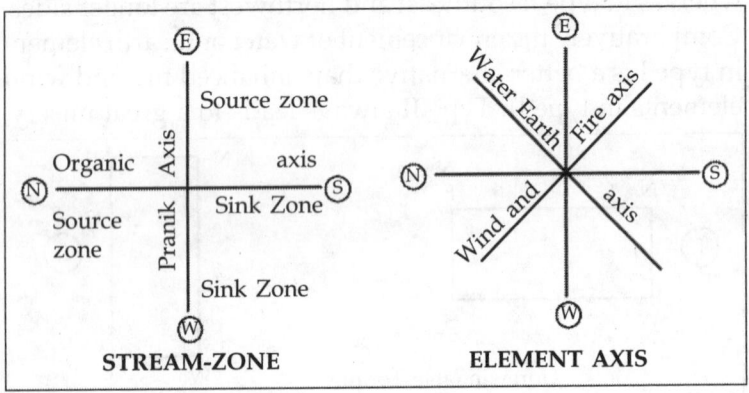

Figure 9.9

sunrays is a fortunate luxury. Whereas, in tropical countries one tries protection from radiating sunrays. European architecture is related to projecting the house to the sun, whereas architecture in tropical countries should try to protect the house from the sun.

Basically in the northern continental area, organic energy is ample, so any loss of organic energy while planning, does not lead to any fault, e.g. as in north light roofs in industrial sheds the "main slopes of roof to south" is a *Mahadosh*, a great fault. But in tropical countries north–south axis is weak; north zones have no potential of organic streams. Scorching sunrays are curbing and radiating from south zones, due to which roof slopes to south which becomes a severe fault, i.e. Mahadosh in energetics of Vaastu. Rather in European countries it is necessary to plan the structure in a way, which can enhance the pranik axis.

Organic axis represents wealth and stability. Pranik axis represents health, habits and intelligence. As in Europe and America, generally a percentage of suicides even in students is more, as the pranik axis is weak. In eastern tradition Prana

---

Effortless gain and smooth progress are the blessings of Vaastu. The huge new construction in Prati Shirdi of Anna chchtra is a remarkable construction based on Vaastu Shastra and is designed by me. The purpose of this place is to feed the devotees, i.e. tranquilising the fire of hunger. A divine form of "fire" a flame lies in the east zone so to get the bliss of divine fire, this structure is made with form that opens out to east, i.e. "C" opening to east, traditionally called "Aaditya-choola". The kitchen is placed in southeast-zone and the structure has north-south-length. Relative south, southwest and west are raised by construction of beautiful magnificent domes. This monumental building has an age-old well to the north zone. All the elements are balanced. Form of the structure is matching to the purpose. Energy streaming is helical. This huge structure got built hardly in a period of 18 months.

is termed as chief deity that emanates the rays of life. The traditional verse says

Pran- Brahmeti -Vyajanat.
Prana is the seed of life.

Due to a good organic axis, mind may go with body, i.e. pleasures and material gains.

Due to a good pranik axis, body and mind travel with intelligence leading to biorhythm.

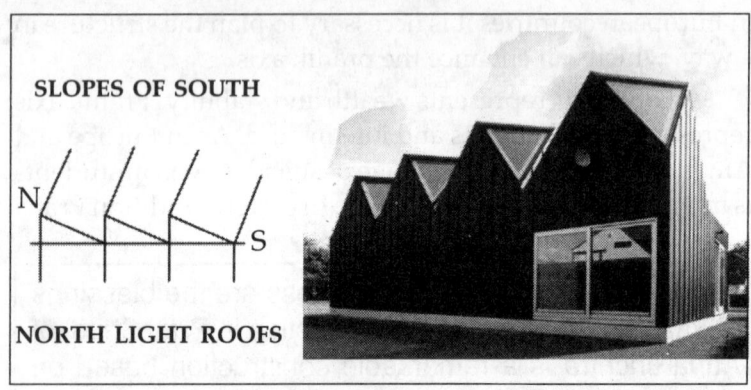

Figure 9.10

Hence tropical countries need planning with improvement in organic streams whereas European countries should give more importance to pranik axis while planning.

l) **Travel of Light:**

Whenever light flows in proper direction, cosmic energy travels in a mandalacar form, i.e. in a logarithmic spiral or a golden ratio. Such energy transforms the voids into spaces, which is the sole purpose of Vaastu Shastra. Whenever light travels from source to sink then it is a natural path, which matches the cosmic reality. Whenever light travels from sink to source then it is not a natural path, hence such light creates disease. In general north, east and ceiling acts as the source zone whereas south, west and flooring acts as the sink zone. In Yogshastra, Sri Dnyaneshwar Maharaj has said this in a wonderful way by saying that Pranancha pranauchi karava transform the pranic energy in a logarithmic spiral called Aum. Transformation of unicolour white light into seven colours is a type of outward expression towards life; hence crystals have immense importance in Vaastu. Each colour represents some specific element and specific planet. Representation of colour is nicely used to realign the qualities of directions. Light is the finest medium to play in every remedy. Vibrations, waves, sound and light are four parameters which are used in Vaastu, Yoga, Astro, Music and Ayurveda. In this four-way pattern, light is the ultimate and final medium. Where there is light, there is a life, but the correct statement will be "where there is a positive confluence of light, there lies "life and god both" as said in Gayatri Mantra: "धियो योन: प्रचोदयात्" Let the intellect dwell in light.

The world famous Yoga authority BKS Iyengar has a yoga institute in Pune that is a marvellous example of Vaastu Shastra. His movement is connected to transformation of personal breath to the virtue of Jal tatwa, i.e. water elements. His yoga institute has a lunar/crescent shape that represents water element, this lunar shape opens out to north, with a good site margin to north. The structure has a slope to north. Every floor on north facade has huge windows. Enhancement of the north flux and loaded southern zone can be observed in all these cases.

PLANETS AND COLOURS	
Sun	Red- Golden
Mars	Red
Mercury	Green
Jupiter	Yellow
Venus	Silver-White
Saturn	Blue- Black
Moon	White-Silver

Norman Foster is considered as the Architect of this Century, whose work is known globally. Hundreds of architects work under his guidance in London. While my lecture in his office,  the following Vaastu tenets were observed. His office is a unique example of correct form, right relation with light and a perfect land, i.e. earth support. This location has a river to north. The famous Thames river being on north zone, the zone is totally enhanced, leading to peace, prosperity and progress. His office has a complete glass facade which enables the presence of north light in the whole office. The double height to north zone has enhanced the virtue of north, whereas single height two floors to south has showered the virtue of earth element. The east west length to the office has got them a variety of projects, e.g. from stadiums to malls and from airport to commercial premises.

ELEMENTS AND COLOURS	
Earth	Yellow
Water	White
Wind	Blue
Fire	Red
Sky	White or colorless

SOURCE AND SINK	
North, northeast, east, northwest and ceiling	Source
Southeast, south, southwest and west	Sink

DIRECTIONS	ELEMENTS	COLOUR
East, Southeast	Fire	Red
South, Southwest	Earth	Yellow
West, Northwest	Wind	Blue
North, northeast	Water	White

Hence if light travels from north to south, it reinforces the organic axis. If light travels from northeast to southwest then it strengthens water-earth axis. If light travels from northwest to southeast then, it strengthens wind-fire axis. All this travel of light from source to sink is a forward positive travel, during which this light showers the chi and bliss to the aspirations of zones. Naturally aspirations flower and contribute the fragrance to the occupants of the house.

In various zones of the house (Ang) this light creates the vibration of prana (Nyas). This prana lights the seed of sound (Mantra-beej), i.e. in traditional language said as

"अंग न्यासोक्त मातरो बीजम्"

When this happens then in the zones of directions, automatically cosmic deities and angles emerge and transform the voids into space, i.e. in traditional language said as

"दिग्बंध देवतास्तत्वम्"

This is the theory of event manifestation, which is the purpose of Vaastu Shastra. Process of event manifestation is based on the expression of aum, i.e. Pranav. Aum is considered a four-legged cosmic word.

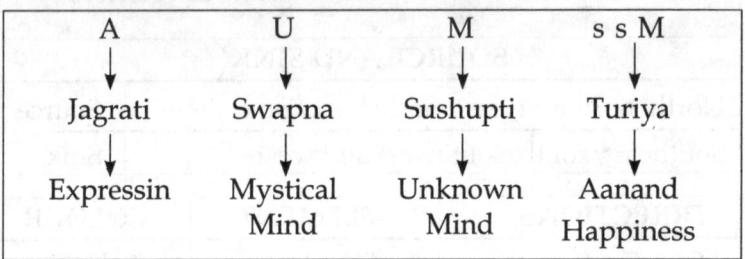

Figure 9.11

In the case of Taj in Mumbai, till there was no load, no obstruction due to the extension of a high rise building to "north", the structure enjoyed the voids and spaces of Rahu, Varun and Nights. The esteem as the "great entertainer and place for business transactions" was beyond the limits. This structure is a Varun choola with "C" opening to west. Traditionally the west zone is called "Rangshala" where Venus also plays an important role. When north got loaded and first time the Saturn came in Leo sign, "all the faults around" gathered the negative momentum and the structure exploded on 26/11.

A to imm is a forward travel from source to sink. Positive expression of life travels like that. It is the mandalacar path along which you meet heavenly deities and bliss. A travel from imm to A will be a reverse gear, a backward journey, a negative expression of life, a travel from sink to source, an anticlockwise path. On this path you meet negative confluence of energies, i.e. voids, ghosts or anti-life element. Yog shastra says the same in different words as, north, northeast and east is governed by

Ida= (Chandra=Moon=Organic) Naadi= (Streams)

One who gets this moon streaming, north, northeast, east streaming, in his life he experiences "a revolution" called as "event manifestation" i.e. "Bhagyakalpa" and he gets strength, stability, peace, bliss and prosperity. south, southwest and west are governed by pingala (Surya or Sun) naadi (streams).

One who gets these south, southwest, west streams, he, in his life experiences friction, blockage and impedance leading to death destructions, demolition, discontinuity and deformation, i.e. travel from imm to A, i.e. a travel from sink to source, i.e. a backward journey. A forward path of energy starts from south-east as a first foot, called Nanda

---

In all such storms and calamities, all those structures which have a perfect form, right surroundings and balanced five great elements will survive with less friction, little blockage and reduced impedance due to a correct cosmic streaming. Aditya choola, i.e. structures with "C" opening to east, Som-choola, i.e. structures with "C" opening to north, Dakshin-pashchim, dvishala, i.e. L opening to northeast and north-south length to the units are some conformed successful forms sanctioned by theory and practice both.

deity. "South-east to south-west to northwest to northeast", i.e. from Nanda Bhadra Jaya to Rikta is a clockwise energy path along which positive events are possible.

> The word Keelak means nailing the carriers of negative energy on the boundary and avoiding their pollution and infections in the main energy zone. Reference of negative energy comes in all the religions, with various forms as black magic, black eyes, vortex, etc. In practical case studies, it has been observed that if form of the space is correct and Kavach, Argala and Keelak rituals are performed then the shield of that space becomes so powerful that the black magic does not work in such a place. The ritual Keelak includes encasing lead rods in south walls/southwest walls and 7 brass rods in the west walls. If the entry is not from south or west then bury 9 steel rods 5'-0" long to south site margin and bury 7 steel rods 5'-0" long to west site margin. This ritual reduces the negative power of Vikat, Putana and Jambuk- which are Vikshep deities of S/SW/W for south zone, we can use the square geometry for burying these rods. For west zone, we can use the circle geometry for burying these rods.

10

MIRACLES AND REALITY

Normally in case studies and consultation there are lot of limitations in executing theoretical constraints. In such cases, at least one should see that source zone should act as source. This means, directions should maintain their characters and virtues to some extent. Even if a small change creates the originality of zones, one starts getting results. It is very difficult to see any space, which has a perfect layout based on Vaastu rules, unless it is planned for. So advice to such units, which already exist, is an art by which without disturbing the machinery layout one has to balance the energy. Many times if the client is not a true believer and good disciple of shastra then he expects a miracle from Vaastu treatment. In such cases Vaastu expert should know the exact nail and its position that pinches your shoe. If this nail is removed then he gets an immediate relief. Once he gets relief, then he will follow all the treatments which will practically change the total frame of energy. At least as a matter of study one should do a study of 100 cases, which have faced problems, or where lockout and total breakdown has happened. Actually these are the spaces where one can learn the real Vaastu Shastra. In Hadapsar industrial estate, Pune, 21 units are locked which have north light roof. Such a probabilistic analysis is necessary.

For example:
1. Out of 28 north light roofs in Hadapsar, Pune, 21 units are locked.

2. Out of 80 units, 60 units in Mahad Industrial estate are closed down due to wrong site selection.
3. Out of 107 units, 100 units are running in full swing at Godrej Industrial estate and 7 units which are south faced are closed or accidents have happened.
4. Enron Project has failed to progress and contribute to to the Nation.
5. In Daman, all units with Nalla to south and west are closed. If one goes in a detailed analysis of above mentioned cases along with its reflection in traditional Vaastu Shastra then he understands some truth.

Let us discuss some practical layouts.

a) Owner : Gogate and Associates
   Place : Bhosari
   Work : Furniture layout

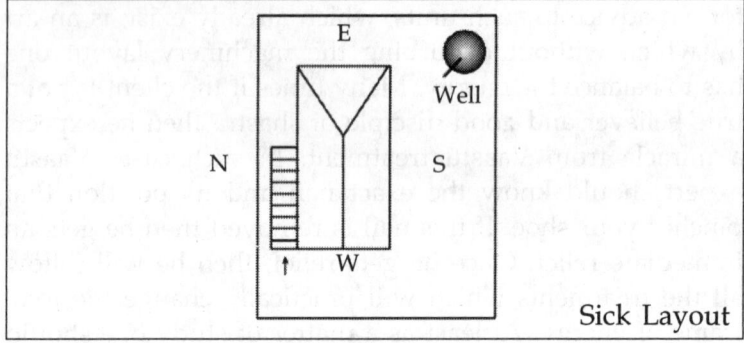

Sick Layout

Figure 10

Position: A unit was facing acute financial shortage with heavy losses and bankruptcy.

1. The unit has east-west length; hence maximum perimeter is projected to the scorching Sun.
2. There was a well in southeast directions which reduced the power of Venus and fire.

3. A staircase in steel to north zone reduced the north site margin and steps go down to west.
4. The entire wooden material was in north and northeast zone which represents water element. "Wood sucks water" as said in feng shui. This had reduced the influx of positive energy.
5. Main entrance to plot being in northwest corner and not in the 4th auspicious division as required. This leads to labour problems and thefts.
6. Site margin to west and south being more than eastand north margin had increased the influx of negative energy.

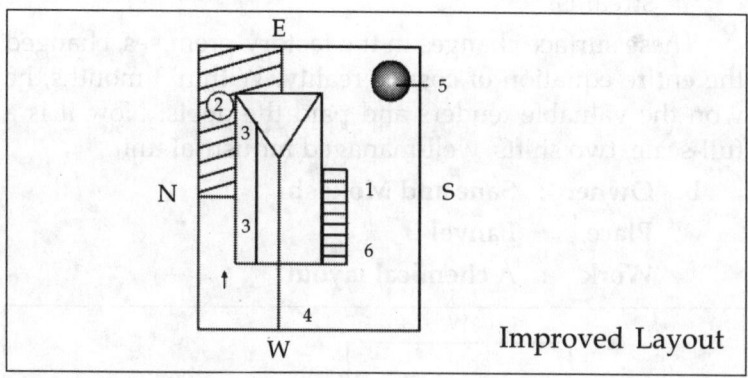

Figure 10.1

Vaastu Treatment

Without going into minute details owner was suggested an external treatment, shown in the figure.

1. A new wooden staircase with steps going high to the west and removal of steel staircase from north zone regulated the energy.
2. North, northeast and part east zone on the ground was reduced to -7'0" level.
3. With a water pool effect and deep depression. This compensated for the large south and west site margin.

4. North side roof was supplied with transparent sheets, so that light travels from north to south, i.e. source to sink. This changes the entire equation of energetics.
5. Main entrance to factory needed a shift to 4th auspicious division, i.e. a sacred cut. Automatically this position made a clockwise path towards the factory.
6. The southeast well was refilled by stones and concrete with a proper ritual and Muhurta.
7. South, southwest, west zone was loaded by stones and raw materials to absorb the negative Pingala streams.

These surface changes in the factory premises, changed the entire equation of cosmic reality. Within 3 months, he won the valuable tenders and paid the debts. Now it is a full-scale, two shifts, well-managed industrial unit.

b. Owner : Sane and Mokashi
   Place : Panvel
   Work : A chemical layout

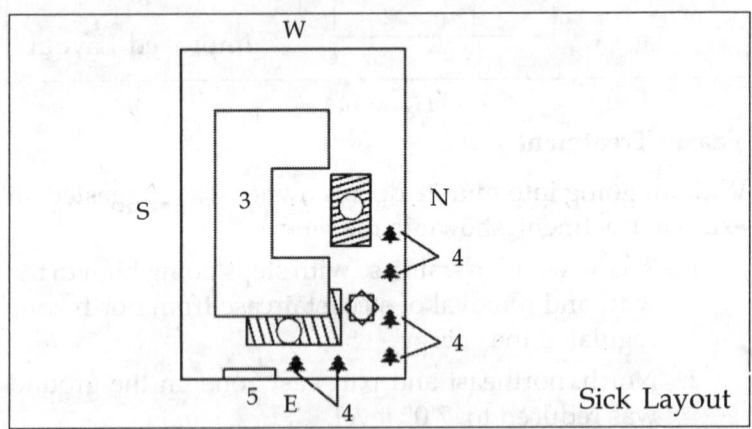

Figure 10.2

Position: When I entered the premises for consultation, the owners were greatly distressed due to no-work condition.

They had a staff of 150 engineers, skilled workers, marketing division and labour. Irrespective of the presence and guidance of a well-qualified Mr. Sane and an experienced engineering expert like Mokashi, the unit was lagging in many areas.

Vaastu Results

1. A towering sprinkler painted black, height 12'0" and diameter 6'0" to northeast zone.
2. Heavy machinery and machine foundations are in central north zone.
3. A central south zone with only a ground floor structure and adjacent right and left arms that are two-storied.
4. North/northeast and east zone with almond trees.
5. Main entrance to right side.
6. A huge canopy to northeast and east zone.

Kamika-Aagam, one of the oldest text on Vaastu Shastra, has defined Vaastu, the superscience and supertechnique as: ''वास्तुतंत्रे महातंत्रे शिवशक्तीसमोदये''

In all the spiritual techniques, it is the movement related to Shiva and Maya is denied. In all the worldly movements the Shiva is denied and whole play is related to Maya. Vaastu is a supertechnique as it gives equal importance to the Shiva and Shakti, i.e. Maya. In Vaastu, elements represent the Shiva, whereas streaming of energy is the play of Shakti, i.e. Maya. Interdependence of energy and elements is the theme of Vaastu Shastra. Many times there is a change of role of both entities. This change of roles make the Vaastu as a mystique subject. Right excitation of elements support the streaming of energy whereas unless there is correct streaming on a helical path, elements do not emerge with full strength. This understanding of interdependence of two dimensions, two entities, is deeply followed in all the processes of Vaastu Shastra.

Vaastu Treatment

Without going into minute details the owner was suggested with external treatments as shown.

1. Since northeast is moon-water element area, a huge black-coloured structure represents a Saturn in northeast creating a *Sade-Sati- effect*. To main source direction acts like moon-Saturn confluence creating poisonous effect to moon. So just lustrous silver paint instead of black was suggested to transform Saturn characters in to moon-water virtues. They were also recommended to lay a white marble in the surrounding zone with, 100 Pearls and 50gm Silver buried below this marble. This flooring and Silver colour changed the entire scenario and character of the zone with acceleration to moon streams. Nostrils of Vaastu Purusha were cleansed and the Prana started vibrating all nodes in its cosmic body. This treatment alone changed the energy equations in the factory.

2. Load of machinery andraised plinth of machinery in the central north zone creates a load and obstruction to organic streams. Moon stream or Chi gets absorbed at the beginning in the huge gravitational load, creating many voids and dying aspirations in further parts of the factory. This obstruction was immediately removed and was substituted by a lunar-shaped water body with crystals, pearls and white marble flooring. This treatment maintained the source characters of north zone. In addition, due to water element and depression north started streaming with forward force to moon streams.

3. The factory had a versatile "C" shaped opening to north, with fault of low structure in central south zone. This got rectified by a pyramidal roof over the slab with towering effect over entire layout. The

characters of pyramid are to hold, to cut, to curtail, to sink and to fire. Pyramids act like Saturn and hence should be used only in south and west zones, i.e. sink zones to control the Sun streams, to curtail the Pingala streams and to hold the fire. South high with pyramids and north low by lunar-shaped water body is a complete cosmic form similar to the *Shivling* leading to essence and bliss of *Satyam Shivam and Sundaram* in the surrounding spaces.

South high by oval shape. North low with flowing water. Cosmic perfect form, "Shiv-linga-Kruti".

Pyramidal towering to South.
Lunar-shaped water body to North.

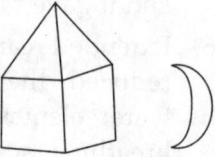

Figure 10.3

4. Christmas tree and almond tree are highly objectional to north, northeast and east zone as, they absorb the organic and Pranik streams, along with that they cast a shadow in the breathing zone of Vaastu. A pyramidal shape of Christmas and almond trees creates vortex of cosmic energy, in the source zone of Vaastu. If they are planted in source zone this creates cosmic gap to north and east zone. Due to this cosmic energy cannot progressively move forward by creating voids, vortex and black hole in the living spaces. On other directions as a matter of treatment to control the Sun streams, to reduce the high temperature and to ignite the cosmic fire

of south by wood, these pyramid-shaped trees are used to south and west zone. The first rectification, these plants were shifted to southwest zone.

5. Main entrance not being at a sacred cut that is 4th division or moon division, this factory suffered a fire hazard, small explosion of coal and leakage of acids. Since the entry is a cut in the southeast zone, with result given in traditional Vaastu as *Ati-krodh and Hani*, i.e. shooting anger and losses. This entry creates anticlockwise path while going from plot to factory, Utsang Pravesh the traditional Sutra says उत्संगारव्ये प्रदेशस्यात् प्रजाहानि: कुटुंबिन:

"Where there is anticlockwise entry, there lies loss of life due to accident" In tradition the other name for this entry is "Heen Bahu Pravesh. Hence rectification of entrance to fourth auspicious division gave two positive effects, viz. it gave clockwise entry and it gave sacred moon division.

6. Extended canopies to northeast, east zone, had reduced the open area of Pranic energy and water element, as if creating a shadow over the breathing spaces. Due to this protective canopy, owner used to keep his total parking in this zone. Vehicles due to "load and steel content" represent a blockage and impedance to the forward streaming of energy, if they are parked in the source zone like north, northeast and east sectors. Vehicles are representatives of Saturn due to steel as the main element. Saturn in north, northeast, east zone shrinks the source characters, contracts the forward streaming and creates the voids, black holes in the source zone. When these canopies were removed the morning Sun rays purified the entire entrance hall and factory.

Aditya of east and *Isha* of northeast became active in a cosmic way on the energy net of the factory.

These six simple changes without any change in machinery layout created a revolution in the energetics of Vaastu. A simple technique of making north, northeast, east as source in character, along with making south, southwest, west as sink in character is the key to improve the Vaastu. After these changes, a fantastic progress forced them to purchase 5 acres of land in Pune region to expand the scope and to enhance services.

c) Owner : Kirloskar and Others
   Place : Pune
   Work : Pneumatic Engineering

Position

1. Unit has north-south length with north light roofs. North light roofs have predominant slope to south, so the spaces are projected to the heat, by major slope of roof projecting to scorching Sun. This is a common cause of hindrance in factory. It is very difficult to treat such roofline.
2. Double floor mezzanine structures in some end bays of north and midways had blocked the organic streams of north zone.
3. All-important cabins have south flux with north blocked situation.
4. North was blocked due to heavy plants with loads of scraps and dead wall.

Vaastu Treatment

In big empires, it is very difficult to execute the Vaastu concept, due to disbelief, controversies and difference of opinions. In such cases by giving importance to hygiene, light and cleaning of source zones one can start getting positive results. Once the positive happening starts, it leads to positive events. Many times when working spaces are improved, this gives immediate relief to the workers, labour-r and skilled people due to availability of better light and ventilation.

1. Initially every bay of industrial workshop was suggested for a transparent sheet to relative east zone of roof. This brought lot of Pranik energy in working space. Whenever light enters from north and east zone it does not raise the temperature of the space but, adds the Prana to voids. This breaks the negative energy loops of south slope. Along with these west zone gives a confinement by reducing the west ventilation. People have a mind block to open the west ventilation because they do not know that a direct wind from southwest and west carries the virus, which creates unhygienic spaces. In tropical countries, west has some raise, high thermal waves and stream of subatomic particles which leads to all types of malignancies, disorders and disagreements. In Vaastu principles west has wind and Varuna elements. It is a sink zone of Pranik energy to enhance the cosmic wind, use of blue colour window glass and use of metal elements in west spaces is advised.

2. Mezzanine in the north and midways creates a fear complex and dullness in the environment due to blockage of north stream. Removal of these floors,

---

The ideal zone for the main cabin is always in the south or southwest zone with face of the main person to north. The second important feature is that this zone should get the distant north light which represents the flowering of distant remote possibilities. The side marble with lunar shape. The side table should have black, brown or yellow colour top of such cabins don't have any north or east light them this south/southeast earth element makes oneself dull, idle and diseased. So along with zone, the streaming of energy has equal importance.

removed the load and burdens of working spaces by adding organic streams and Pranik feel. Free streaming of energy from source to Sink, from north to south and from east to west is the soul of Vaastu Shastra. This one treatment can bring a great relief. Removal of these floors increased the sky element in the factory, which affected a mandalacar streaming of energy.

3. Chairman, Directors and top executives had cabins to south zone with lot of light from south. A long corridor to N-zone, but closed N along with max light from "S" disturbed the energetics of this main vital area of the factory. South zone is good provided south is closed, confined, loaded and is getting a breath from north and east zone, otherwise south zone is called a zone of romance in traditional Vaastu Shastra. This being the zone of Pingala, Sun streams, it activates fragmentation, decay and degeneration. Whenever a normal Sunlight enters from south zone, it is in opposite direction to the natural organic streams, which travels from north to south. Vaguely one can say that light from south is a hindrance and opposition to the electromagnetic flux. It creates a negative confluence with the electromagnetic flux. In traditional language it is a negative confluence of Jaivik and Pranik energy that is Prana in opposition to the Jeeva, i.e. a death penalty in a cosmic way. Whenever light emanates from south, then south becomes a source zone which is against its natural characters. When sunlight travels from south then being white in colour, its virtue is of Jal-Tatwa.

White =	Water =	*Jal*
Red =	Fire =	*Agni*
Yellow =	Earth =	*Pruthvi*
Blue =	Wind =	*Pawan*

This is classified as "Gun-Varnan" of five great elements. This white colour light being of water element, reduces the fire of southeast and south zone and in turn reduces the virtue of south zone. South zone is equated to the Mars for the strength that represents a fire element. So whenever light emanates from south, it reduces the commanding quality of mars. Use of yellow glass to the south window stabilizes the zone by pruthvi-tatwa. Use of copper article in south zone accelerates the strength of Mars. Lunar-shaped white marble top to the table enhance the moon characters of north zone. A stone pedestal to southwest zone gives stability of Pruthvi-Tatwa and paralyses the divisive activity of sun streams. An opening north wall by glass panels or glass bricks creates streaming of north zone in the office spaces.

Loads of scrap garbage and heavy plantation was removed from north zone leading to better streaming characters to north zone. Additional borewells to the north zone in a lunar geometry, did wonders due to deep depressions to the north zone. Use of white marble pearls, crystals and silver can work magic if used properly to north zone. A lunar shape has better qualities of water element, i.e. Jal-Tatva. Additional borewells effectively create sloping ground profile to north and raised south zones. Acceleration and strength to moon streams/organic streams/source streams/ida streams is the main principal of Vaastu Shastra, which happens due to treatment like lunar shapes, white marbles, pearls, crystals, depressions and water bodies.

These four simple changes created a virtuous change in spaces, leading to an ordered cosmic breath in working areas. Skilled workers and labourers could breathe better, which was a refreshing change for them, leading to a better creative understanding in everyday working. Anybody entering this zone, after these changes, was amazed and thanked the managing directors. This encouraged progress in share value of the company.

d) Owners : Valke and Associates
   Place : Selvassa-Gujrat
   Work : Automotive parts-assembly

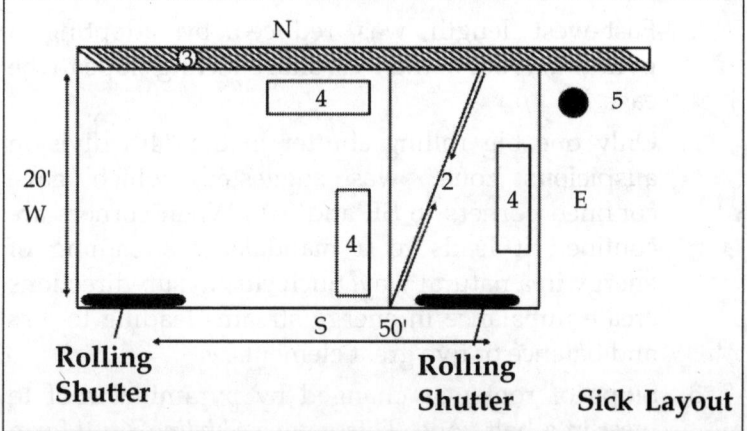

Figure 10.4

Position: This miracle is related to a very small space of 1000 sq ft, small unit of a simple person. Many times people think that this shastra is needed only for very rich establishments, but this example of 1000 sq ft will change their minds. A treatment was done in 2001. Now in 2005, we are working for expansion of this factory into 15,000 sq ft work area. This miracle could happen due to new relations and equations of cosmic energy in a 1000 sq ft small work area.

Vaastu Reasons

1. Unit has E-W length.
2. Rolling shutters are in the corner leading to voids to SW and SE zones.
3. Entire roof slope was to the south.
4. Positions of lathe machines was in northeast and central zone.
5. A huge Peepal tree was casting a big shadow from east zone.

6. Entire N is closed due to the adjoining unit to the north side.

Vaastu Treatment

1. East–west length was reduced by adopting a pyramidal roof to the west side effecting slope to the east.
2. Only one big rolling shutter in the "4th division auspicious zone" was suggested, which gave confined corners to SE and SW. When corners are confined it leads to a mandalacar streaming of energy in a natural way. Such cuts to sub-directions create imbalance in energy streams leading to loss and balance of five great elements.
3. Slope of roof was changed by pyramidal roof to west in a half zone. This gave a *Shivling Kruti* form to roof, so that the powerful element sky gave a cosmic rhythm to the entire space. Along with these changes, transparent sheets to N and E zone forced the light to travel from N to S and from E to W, in other words from source to sink.
4. Machinery layout with load to south, southwest and west gave a correct energy-matter equation. Loads to S/SW/W leads to absorption of Pingala sun streams. Removal of loads from N and E zone, enhanced the activity of moon-organic streams.
5. Cosmic balance is attained by Peepal tree in west zone, so removal of this tree from east zone enhances the scope of pranik energy. In traditional Vaastu Shastra, shadow in aura zone of Vaastu, of anything is considered as inauspicious.
6. A simple trick of depressions to N accelerated the organic streams. In addition a treatment of white marble pearls, crystals and silver in depression zone enhances the virtue of organic water element zone.

These changes in factory shed, entirely changed the cosmic equations leading to a mandalacar streaming of cosmic breath, which accelerated the forward time energy curve and the aspiration started pouring bliss in spaces. Soon in a two years period, positive changes happened.

e) Owners : Panhale and others
   Place : Bhosary- Pune
   Work   : Mechanical engineer

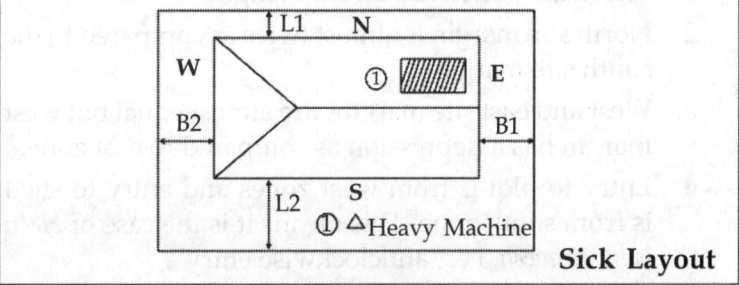

Sick Layout

Figure 10.5

In many factories, it is not possible to change the roofs or machinery layouts, positions of boilers, high-lows of the land, or zones of the buildings. In such a situation, if the main cabin of chairman, vice chairman or directors are rectified on the principles of Vaastu, then often miracle happens and they experience a radical change in the market possibilities. The ideal proportion of a cabin is in the "golden ratio with north-south as the length". Distant clear north light is like an assurance of success. If such a light is not available then try to provide a sky light in the north zone. White marble flooring to relative north and east, alongwith Jaisalmer yellow stone flooring to relative south and southwest zone, assures the elements and energy streaming. Stone cladding to south, southwest walls, gives virtues of the earth element. One solid gold-plated lead pyramid in southwest corner assures the complete balance of energy matter equation.

This case is a typical example, where "unloading the source zones and reloading to sink zones" has played a great miracle. Nothing good ever happened in this place. The previous owner committed suicide due to bankruptcy. The second owner followed the advice and executed changes and experienced relief.

Vaastu Reasons

1. The factory shed has an E-W length.
2. North site margin is almost twice as compared to the south site margin.
3. West and east site margins are almost equal but west margin has a depression as compared to east zone.
4. Entry to plot is from west zones and entry to shed is from south zone. This means it is the case of *Heen bahu-pravesh*, i.e. "anticlockwise entry".
5. There was a huge machine in northeast zone.

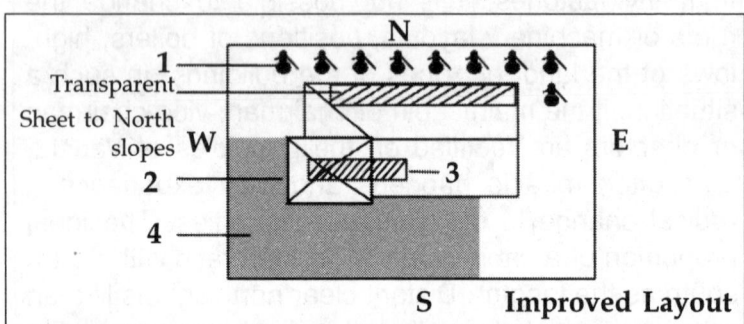

Figure 10.6

Vaastu Treatment

1. Denotes 9 borewells creating extreme depressions to N zone.
2. Pyramidal towering top to SW- zone.
3. Heavy machine shifted to SW zone.

4. SW zone reloaded by raw material.
5. West zone was landscaped by rock garden and Peepal trees.
6. South zone was landscaped by almond and Christmas trees, which have a pyramidal shape.
7. 5 kg lead was buried to central south zone in ascending geometry at nine places.

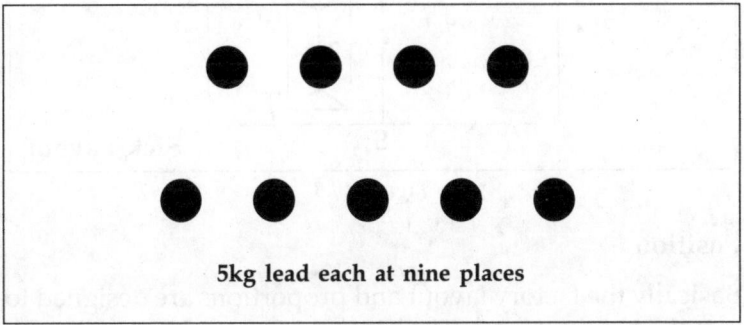

Figure 10.7

All this treatment is surface treatment which changed the energy matter equation in the factory. Additional borewells around 100'0" deep to north side, compensated the fault of excessive south margin. Towering pyramidal top to the southwest roof, curtailed the E-W length effect. Transparent sheets to north roof, forced the Pranik energy to travel along the organic streams. This one treatment, if followed correctly, does wonders in the energetics of Vaastu. Shift of heavy machines to SW zone cleared the path of organic streams. Northeast represents Ish. When this deity starts blessing the spaces, then hindrance ends, friction vanishes and lockage breaks. Borewells to north and reloading the south by lead metal, landscapes and heavy plantations, makes the land rich, prosperous and divine. All the original texts like *May-Matam, Maan Saar, Bruhad Vaastumala, Manushylay-Chandrika* have the same opinion regarding this pattern of earth slope.

f) Owners : Vairagi and others
   Place : Hyderabad- Andhra Pradesh
   Work : Chemical Engineering

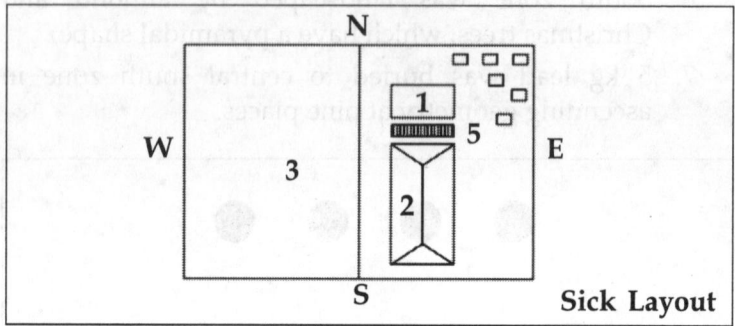

Sick Layout

Figure 10.8

Position

Basically the factory layout and proportions are designed to suit the Vaastu tenets. The plot and factory has N-S length

> The renowned computer scholar and scientist Dr. Vijay Bhatkar's office cabin is a perfect reflection of principles of Vaastu. In the total office premises his placement is in the central south zone, with light energy from north and east directions. The cabin has white marble flooring to the adjoining north and east zone. This cabin has a yellow colour flooring and south/west walls has stone cladding. The yellow colour represents the fertile earth element where the tradition and modernity both have equal balance. Black color represents the distress of earth element, whereas brown colour represents the hardship of earth element. This cabin has "north-south length" which adds virtue to the organic stream. The table top was suggested in white marble with slight lunar shape to the north external face.

with main ventilation from north. Machinery load was properly arranged to south and west zone. Site margins to north are more than south margins, and site margins to east are more than the west margins. Irrespective of all these facts, factory working went in huge losses.

Vaastu Reasons

1. Empty plastic containers of chemical are blue in colour. These empty containers were stacked in north and northeast zone. Not the load but colour played negative role in this case. Since these containers were empty, their load was not the issue. But blue colour emits Saturn effects and wind effects. Saturn shrinks, contracts and diminishes the Aditya and moon qualities. When these empty barrels were rearranged in west zone, immediately N and NE started the streams of organic energy.

There was a charismatic era of Harshad Mehta in the world of finance. His great courage, alertness, clever mind, grip on the market was outstanding. It is interesting to study the house of such a dangerous and clever mastermind. The sea coast to south/southwest/west zone to his house is evident of the tiger on which he was riding. Since north to his house was closed and loaded due to a staircase, so no positive outcome happened in his life. It was a duplex flat with reducing floor from south/SE zone, leading terraces to south/southeast zone. Excessive attack of pingala/sun streams of south/southwest/southeast created a suicidal fire in his personality. A cooling water element of north being absent, the fire got extended to explosion and his mystique death.

2. Due to additional requirement of space, owners purchased the plot adjoining to the west margin. This additional space towards the west acts as the extension to the sink zone. In totality west zone and west margin became unlimited, this changed the entire cosmic equation leading to a huge financial loss.
3. As a matter of requirement, owners constructed additional office premises separate from original layout to north side. Traditional Vaastu clearly mentions this as Kanchan Dwishala — which leads to wealth losses.

Vaastu Treatment

1. Rearranging the blue containers to northwest and west zone, the effect of excessive west margins was removed.
2. Use of plants, lead and landscapes to the west side readjusted the effects of new plot purchase to west side.
3. Additional improvement to virtues of north streams by borewells, white marble silver, pearls and crystals readjusted the effect of Kanchan Dwishala pattern.
4. Acid tanks to the north zone are good as regards the depression, but acid being of Agni-Tatwa, fire element, are not suitable in north zone. So by maintaining the depression to north, additional pits to keep the acid tank were reorganised to east.

This gave a proper cosmic befitting to the planet element — direction classification.

1. Kanchan- Dvihsala new office.
2. NS length to original unit.
3. Additional plot purchased to west side.
4. Placement of empty blue barrels.
5. Underground acid tanks to N-W zone.

g) Owner : Khangal and others
   Place : Nasik
   Work : Mechanical/Electrical engineering

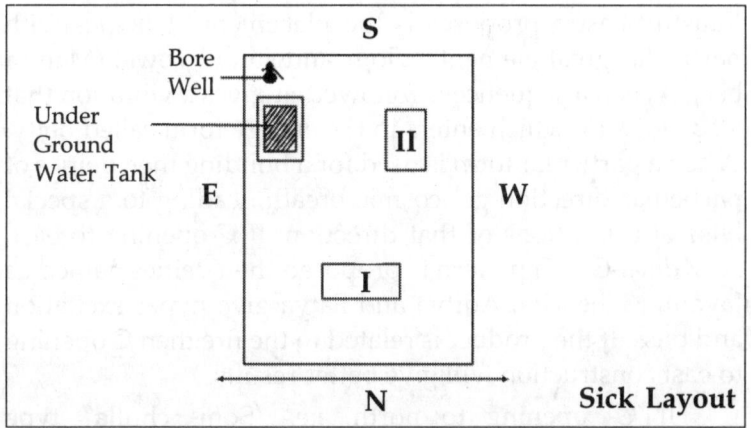

Figure 10.9

The treatment Kavach includes fixation of deities, planets and elements. This is achieved by a ritual called as "Ratnadhyay". It is a mystique ritual connected to deities, aura and particular zones of the plinth. The auspicious stone acts as a Yang seed implanted in the Yin body of the earth in a way that it acts as the "Tai-Chi", i.e. complete balance of zone, aspiration and elements. A correct placement of auspicious stones limits the boundaries of a plot and the vast sky energy starts radiating in the virtues of earth through the medium of directions. It is the miniature reflection of the solar system in the limited grid of the house. It is the ritual that connects and relates the microcosm of the house to the macrocosm of solar system. This ritual demarcates the energy channels and sutra devta in the Vaastu.

This is a typical case where fault is related to five great elements, sequence of construction and particular form of Vaastu. This is a cosmic mystical problem where aura and deities have a great importance. The 81 grid analysis which Vaastu Shastra proposes is the placement of deities with particular great element, colour and sound vowel (Mantra beej). When a sequence is followed, it gives a vibration that leads to aura, which enters in the energy form called deity. When a particular form is used for a building then deities of particular direction get cosmic breath, leading to a special bliss of aspirations of that direction. If C-opening to east, i.e. *Aditya-Choola* pattern is proposed then deities named as Jayant, Mahendra, Aditya and Satya give hyper excitation and bliss. If the product is related to the fire then C opening to east construction will give better results.

If C- opening to north, i.e. "Som- chulla" type construction is proposed then particularly deities named as Bhallat, Som and charak give hyper excitation and bliss. If the product is related to water element then C- opening to N construction will give better results.

Vaastu Reasons

1. A borewell and underground water tank to southeast zone is a paradox as regards fire element and depression. Southeast should be always high as compared to northwest. So depression to southeast creates a severe fault.
2. The 1st building is in north and 2nd building is in west, this means the south and southeast is void, without any load. Traditional Vaastu says that sequence of construction must be from southeast as "Prathmeshtika" Nanda, i.e. first form on plot. Rest of the construction is to be completed in a clockwise direction ending in northeast at last. If sequence of construction is followed as per the theory then it creates a mandalacar streaming of energy.

3. Site margin to north is very small due to which vibration of north deities is missing, so the prosperity and progress are missing.

Vaastu Treatment

1. Refilling the southeast boring by sand and performing the ritual named as "Koop-shanti" was suggested. Underground water tank was also refilled by stones and concrete. Four red coral on proper *Muhurat* to be buried in southeast zone was a supplementary suggestion.
2. Reconstruction of "missing southeast arm" is a must. A pyramidal roof to this arm gave wonderful results. Before this construction a cosmic ritual called as "Ratnadhyay" and "Dhatuadhyay" reduces the possibility of any accident or lag in happening. Southeast is a zone of Venus and fire, unless these deities are compensated, no action leads to a positive fruit. A proper plantation and landscapes to southeast and south is necessary before the start of construction of this arm.
3. Additional boring to north zone to compensate the reduced construction site margin of north and use of silver, pearls, crystals to accelerate the vibration of north deities will give better and early results.

After completing all the remedies mentioned above, the owner got astonishing results, not only in India, but also abroad.

11

Cosmic Remedies of Eight Directions

a. East zone:- This zone represents the fire element with deities as Mahendra, Aditya and satya. This is a source direction of pranik energy. In Ratnadhyay, stones related to mars Red Coral is suggested for inner faces and Vajra, and diamond is suggested representing the deity Indra for outer space. Plant suggested is vat, i.e. Banyan tree. Mars and Indra, both representing strength, power, ambition and confidence. Aditya represents intelligence, tradition and progressive life. East zone is represented by 1/5/9, i.e. Aries, Leo and Sagittarius signs. Whenever in a house, factory, office and plot, east has many faults, then as and

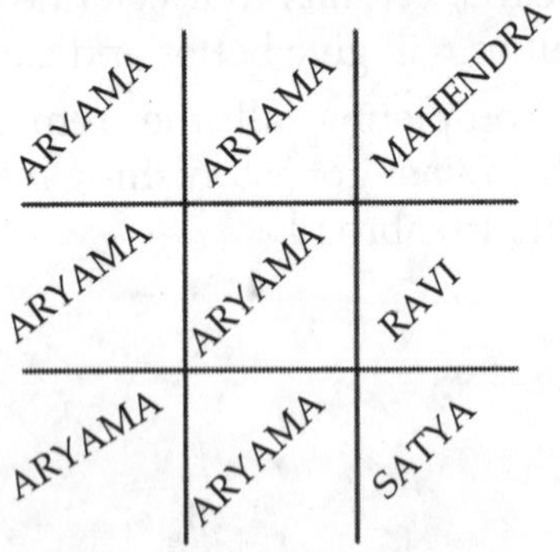

ARYAMA	ARYAMA	MAHENDRA
ARYAMA	ARYAMA	RAVI
ARYAMA	ARYAMA	SATYA

Deities of East Zone

Figure 11

when Saturn and Rahu enter to 1/5/9, i.e. Aries, Leo and Sagittarius, then this is the period that bad event may hit that house, office or factory. Along with Mars and Sun, who are representative of the east zone, if go in the negative confluence, then the severity of bad event increases in this period. An additive cosmic remedy should be done to east zone to reduce the power of evil energy; or one should treat north zone to dilute this evil energy; or one should add virtues to the west zone.

Since Vaastu acts as a two-stream theory, any axial improvement helps to improve the effect, i.e. northeast = southwest/northwest = southeast/east = west/north = south. These are complementary directions. Any improvement in northeast gives better result to southwest. Any improvement to northwest gives better results to southeast. Any improvement in west, gives better results to east. Improvement in east can be done by using copper, silver, wood, red coral, crystals, and mirrors. Improvement in west can be done by using bronze, white metal, silver, lead as metals, blue crystal as stones, emeralds and sapphires as stones, statues, landscape, blue lights and heaviness to zone. Whenever east is closed, loaded, dirty, polluted, raised and less, then such a situation creates faults in east. Whenever

---

Whenever light travels from "north to south" or "east to west" it reinforces the virtue and quality of entire space. When proper elements are established in the zones, it leads to stability and right momentum in the space. So a simple remedy is to provide transparent sheets in roof in the N and E zone of any factory. This simple correction will create the streaming from N to S and E to W, i.e. from source to sink. A second simple correction in the factory shed could be to apply blue colour to the west zone and yellow colour to the south zone of the roof.

west is void, sloping, depressed and more ventilated then such a situation creates faults in west. Regarding industries, faults in east lead to low working energy, less appreciation, reduces imagination, no recognition stage of saturation, problems related to fire element hardships, dependency on external factors, loss of indigenous attempts for success, loss of order and discipline.

b. Southeast zone:- This zone represents intense fire element with deities in Vaastu Purusha Mandala as Bhrush, Nabh, Anil, Poosha and Vitatha as Aawaran deities, Savitra as Anga-deity and Vidari as Vikshep–deity. Whenever fire is dormant in this zone, it provides warmth leading to positive expression of Anga-devta-savitra. Whenever fire is absent or intense in this zone then the Vikshep- devta Vidari becomes active, leading to all negative events.

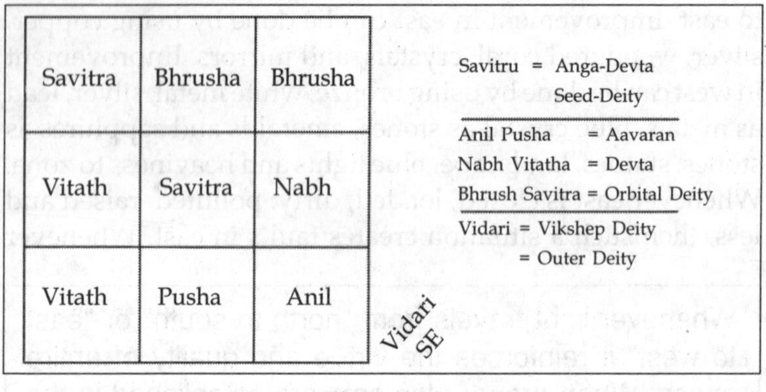

Savitra	Bhrusha	Bhrusha
Vitath	Savitra	Nabh
Vitath	Pusha	Anil

Savitru = Anga-Devta
Seed-Deity

Anil Pusha = Aavaran
Nabh Vitatha = Devta
Bhrush Savitra = Orbital Deity
Vidari = Vikshep Deity
= Outer Deity

Vidari SE

Figure 11.1

To avoid the activation of Vidari, even a red flower tree is not allowed to southeast zone. The colour red is a direct expression of fire element that should not be present. In Ratnadhyay using yellow Sapphire as the seed of positive light increases the power of Anga-devta. The power of Vidari is retaliated by using red coral in the outer system. Intense fire elements can be controlled by earth element, without reducing the power of fire. Rather earth element can transform the explosive characters of fire in to warmth and nourishing virtue. Hence in traditional Vaastu Shastra, southeast should be raised, without depression and water. Moment the land slopes to southeast, the Savitra deity loses the contact with Brahma, leading to activation of the outer deities, viz. Vidari. One Mango tree in the outer zones of southeast can control the activation of Vidari. Use of red coral and copper pyramids can curtail the rise of Vidari.

Whenever southeast is polluted, has a red expression, or has depression and water body or has cut and extension, then the activation of Vidari and silent mode of Savitra disturbs the peace and cosmic order. This leads to accident, explosion, loss of energy, disorder and loss of wealth. Fire, i.e. Agni is called as mouth of all deities, so disturbed fire zones end the aspect divine cosmic order. Loss of warmth and heat of fire leads to end of life in traditional Vaastu Shastra; everything begins with southeast and so it is called as Prathmeshtika-Nanda. In an industrial set-up, all exothermic processes, acid base processes, controlled explosion, all patterns of powers should be organised to southeast zone but with right expression of earth element, to control and create the right dialogue with fire element.

c. South zone:- This zone needs a powerful earth to control the exploding fire. That's why in astrology, this zone is represented by 2/6/10, i.e. Taurus, Virgo and Capricorn signs which represent the earth element. This is a sink direction of organic energy. In Ratnadhyay Ketu's stone, cat's eye is used as a substitute to mars, with qualities of curtailing and cutting the energy waves. Ketu- stone is used for the inner spaces and in the outer sky to contract the energy waves and to stabilize the fire blue Sapphire of Saturn is suggested. Stabilization of volcanic strokes of fire elements is suggested by planning the Audumber tree in south zone. In feng shui, element for south is fire, due to the environmental conditions in China. In China, north, northeast and east zones are polluted because of dusty chilly

```
        VIVASWAN | VIVASWAN | VIVASWAN
        VIVASWAN | VIVASWAN | VIVASWAN
        GANDHARYA | YAMA | GRIHAKSHAT
```

Deities of South Zone

Figure 11.2

winds carrying Siberian yellow dust. In China due to low thermal levels, sun is used as the warmth element, whereas in tropical countries like India the whole architecture is knitted to protect from the scorching sun. Constraints of south in feng shui and Vaastu are different as regards the position of sun and climatic conditions. Deities of south are Gandhrva, Yam Grahkshat and Vivswan. So far as Vivswan is connected to the Brahma, south zone does not give negative results. Whenever south slopes, with raised north, Vivswan does not get the Prana and outer vast south spaces start their activation, leading to chaos in the energetics of the

---

It is the science that transforms the voids into spaces. It fills the gap between the cup and leaps, so that in life one enjoys the comfort, creativity and connectivity of their own free will and blissful choice. By balancing the five great elements, it creates the aura of balanced planets around the person and house, so that oneness of mind and intelligence always leads to right action in life. Tuning of breath, unification of mind and intelligence and right choices in life being the real gift of this science so this science is called as "Sthapaty-Veda".

inner spaces. Hence towering structures and chimneys and raised platforms to south zone, maintain the equilibrium of energy. Godrej industrial estate in Vikroli-Mumbai has given very good results to all the residing units due to high raised steel tanks to south zone and roads progressing to north. A divine form of Shivling Kruti is naturally formed here due to this geometry.

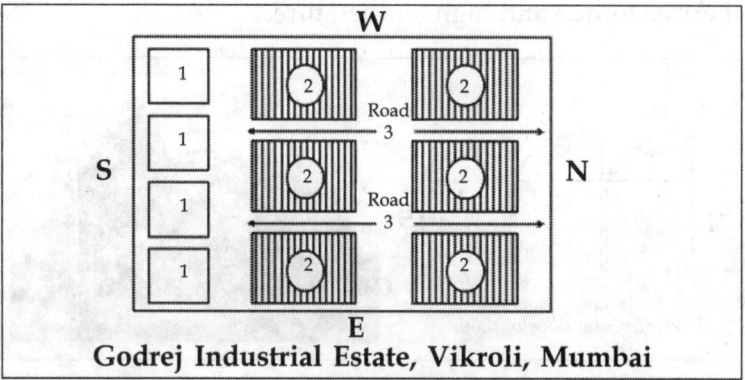

Godrej Industrial Estate, Vikroli, Mumbai

Figure 11.3

The word "Argala" is connected to the energy that gives prosperity. Hence all the rituals related to north zone means presenting Argala, i.e. energy to the space. The element of north is water that spreads as the prosperity. By alloting one extra division to Jal tatva in Nabhi ritual, already the process of Argala begins. Virtues of water element are expressed with pearls, crystal, silver, white light, depression, lunar shapes, mirrors and white marble. Whenever light falls on the water face, light gets polorised. Crystals and white marble have the same virtue of polorising the light. Whenever all the above characters get clubbed to north zone, to create the source element in the north direction the ritual of Argala gets completed. It is preferable to do all north corrections on the "Monday morning" as the Muhurtha, the most auspicious time.

1. Raised towering steel tanks to "S".
2. Industries in east-west axis.
3. Roads along north-south axis.

Whenever industries have north light roof structures, roofs have main slope to south. So the roof surface sloping to south, projects the entire roof to the scorching sun, leading to loss of bio-magnetism attached to the spaces, due to high thermal torque and high temperature.

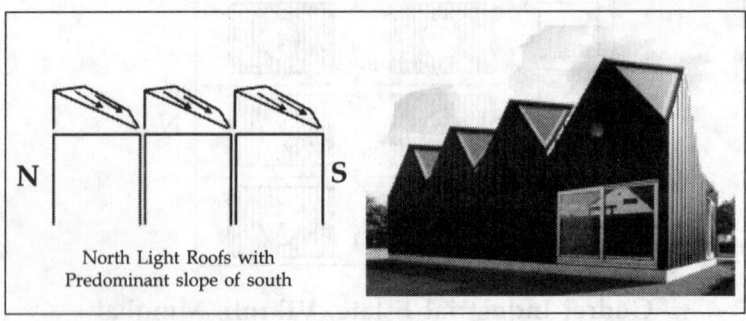

Figure 11.4

In these type of structures, outer spaces, like Vikshep Devta, becomes hyperactive leading to all types of failure, accidents and discontinuity.

d. Southwest zone:- In Vaastu and feng shui both this is a zone of Pruthvi-Tatwa. Stability, fertility and continuity

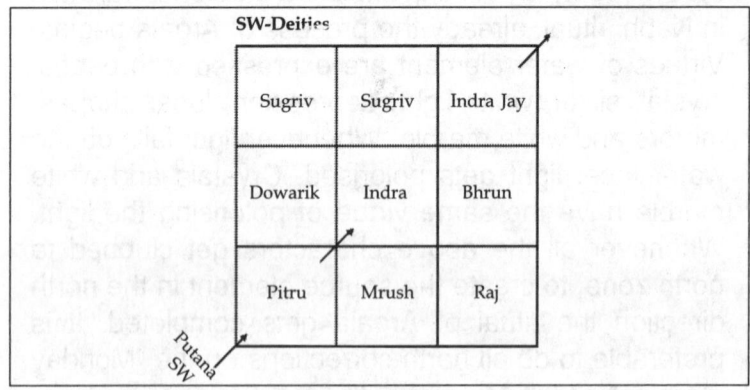

Figure 11.5

are the virtues of Pruthvi- Tatwa. If south-west is high then all water streams to north and east. In traditional language they are called as Utter Vahini and Poorva Vahini and are considered as the divine waters. Heavy machines; raised platforms; black, blue, brown, yellow colours; raised towering structures; pyramidal forms; hills give excellent results if they are placed in this zone, Astrologically crystals—sphatik representing Indra and Yellow Sapphire representing Pruthvi-Tatwa are used to create the cosmic virtues in earth.

Deities of this zone are Sugriv, Douvarik, Pitru, Mrush, Brungraj, Indra and Indrajay. Indra acts at the core of the direction, surrounded by rest of deities. In outer spaces the Putana-Vikshep devta resides. When the sphatik-crystal is placed in the division of Indra, Anga-devta gets the cosmic power and gets connected to Brahma automatically. When yellow Sapphire is placed in the outer spaces, it absorbs the poison of Vikshep- devta- Putana and protects the energetics of inner spaces. This zone is a discharging zone and is related to Apan Vaayu. In Yogshastra, Surya Naadi, i.e. right breath activates the Apan vaayu. Hence all types of discharging processes should be arranged to this zone in various industrial activities. If this zone is not connected to the central core, i.e. Brahmasthan to its relative northeast, then all types of idleness, inactivity and inability disturb the working in this zone. If important persons like chairman, directors find their cabins here and these cabins are devoid of north and east streams, then these important persons lose their grace, charisma and prestige. Very soon they become targets of criticisms and face the loss of popularity. In short, in all zones and sectors, if connectivity to central zone is lost then aspiration of that direction does not shine and prosper. In Ratnadhyay this connectivity gets established in a cosmic way through placement of gems in central zones.

e. West zone: -This zone represents the sink direction of Pranik energy. Asur, Pushpadant and Varuna are the surface deities of this zone and Mitra forms the inner core of west zone.

DEITIES OF WEST ZONE

ASUR	MITRA	MITRA
VARUNA	MITRA	MITRA
PUSHPADANTA	MITRA	MITRA

Figure 11.6

Jambok is the Vikshep deity of this zone. Whenever roof, ground slopes to west, means east is high, then the core deity Mitra loses the connection with central "Brahma". In such a case Jambok Vikshap deity becomes active leading to disagreement in every walk of life. In the industrial world, west represents partners, legal and court matters. So fault in west zone will lead to quarrels and misunderstanding in partners, complications in court matters, and loss of property. In feng shui, west represents metal element. In Indian astrology west is represented by Saturn and Venus so iron and silver could be good metals to flower the aspiration of west. In Ratnadhyay, west is equated to the blue Sapphire and outer spaces are connected, to the green, emerald. Again "Saturn inside and Mercury outside" will continue with "iron and silver" or "iron and bronze" as the metal element. A Peepal plant in Prangan can keep the Jambok – Vikshep deity away from the inner spaces, so that the aura of Mitra, core deity of west, becomes active and the west zone gets the bliss of central Brahma. This is the zone of *Vaayu-Tatwa*, i.e. wind element. Astrologically

3/7/11 signs represent Vaayu-Tatwa=wind element. Lords of 3/7/11 are mercury Venus and Saturn, same logic is used in Ratnadhyay. Raised west, hills to west, less windows and openings to west, steel iron and metal to west, machines to west, towering and chimneys to west, no slopes to west are the virtues that can flower the aspirations of west. In grounds with slopes to west, construction form for the building should be C- opening east, so that Pranik energy gets channelized. This is a powerful remedy to reduce the bad effects of west slopes. Even while giving a slope to the roof provide 1/3 slope to west and 2/3 slope to east so that mainly pranik energy gets the importance.

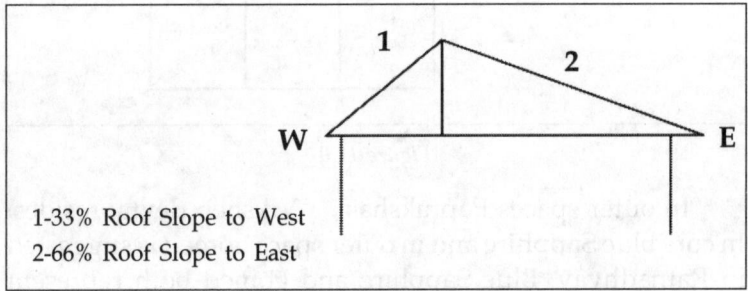

Figure 11.7

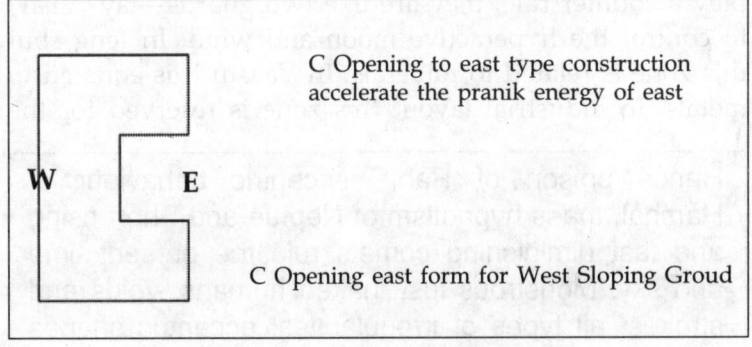

Figure 11.8

f. Northwest zone: - This zone represents the active wind zone. The core deity of this zone is *Rudra,* surrounded by *Mukhya, Rudra jaya, Soash, Papyakshma rog* and *Nag.*

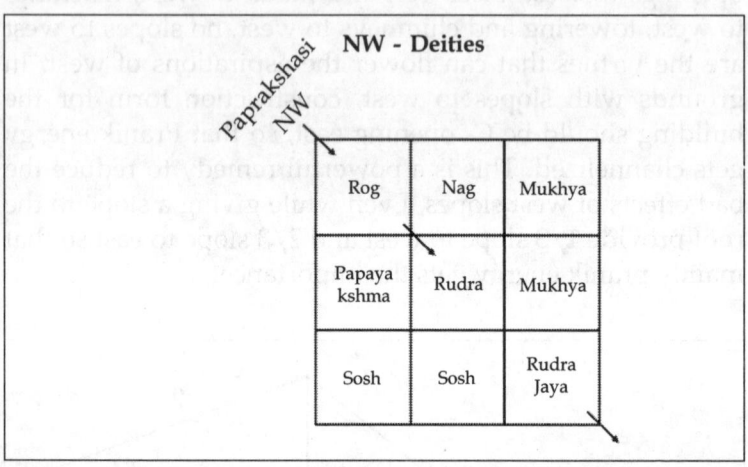

Figure 11.9

In outer spaces Paprakshasi, a Vikshep devta, resides. In core blue Sapphire and in outer space gomed is suggested in Ratnadhyay. Blue Sapphire and gomed both represent very strong negative planets, viz. Saturn and Rahu.

To control the hyperactive wind element; these planets play a counter role, they are like two guards—Jay- Vijay, to control the hyperactive moon and wind. In feng shui this zone is related to minerals. In Vaastu it is equated to metals. In industrial layout this zone is reserved for the

Hence poison of Rahu, eccentric behaviour of Harshal, mass hypnotism of Neptue and Short rising and fast diminishing comets rule the present time and sky. Monstrous lust, naked humans, voids and strokes, all types of irregularities, eccentric shapes and colours, rat race and immoral acts will dictate the world of advertising, media and the architecture.

finished goods. Purity, dignity and sail of finished goods gets accelerated, if the distribution is done in this zone. Since Vaastu Shastra is a two-streams theory, northwest is connected to southeast. Southeast zone should be raised as compared to northwest zone. Since moon controls this zone, any final finished products that remains in this zone, gets the speed of moon. Astrologically moon is a fastest moving planet, which covers each sign in 54 hours. If northwest zone has virtue, then wind attains next dimension of sound. In traditional language Pawan becomes swar as siddhi. Vibrations, waves, sound and light are the four pillars of Vaastu Shastra.

Mandalacar streaming of energy completes this journey of energy and attains the order of light. It is considered as the ultimate goal in spiritual—travel where "Prachodayat" means Divine and Glorious light that removes the darkness from our paths, that we are able to see the way. That's why

> Grid planning is the base of Architecture, whereas dynamic energy grid planning is the base of Indian style of Architecture, i.e. Vaastu Shastra. In modern science the reference of Kari Grid or Heartman's grid of bioenergy is given. This concept has been considered in a much better way in Vaastu Shastra. The whole plot is divided in 9 x 9 i.e. 81 divisions. Each division is separated by a stream of energy of width L/72 or B/72. These energy channels are kept free of any column and beam positions, so that the earths bioenergy is forced to travel in the order and discipline of the house. In traditional Vaastu these are termed as Sutra-Devta viz. Kamala, Sati, Savita, Pranvahini, etc., around the Vaastu Purush Mandala. A profound, immense and intense energy of nature is channellised to stream in the house in a mandalacar form so that home becomes a perfect shield.

one of the dimensions of Vaastu Shastra is a "set of rules that corrects the relation with sun". A positive confluence of Prana and Jeev, i.e. solar and organic streams is the fundamental principle of Vaastu Shastra. In some traditional books, depression and water to this zone is considered good for prosperity and fertility.

In practical understanding, this zone should be clean, lustrous and ordered, Blue and Silver combination of colour suits this direction. Generally metal inlay adds virtue to the zone.

g. North Zone:-. This zone represents the water element with Bhallat, Som, Charak and Pruthvidhar as the deities of north zone. North is a source direction of Jaivik, i.e. organic energy. Green emeralds in the inner spaces and pearls in the outer spaces are suggested in the Ratnadhyay. Irrespective of the position of the sun, this direction remains as the source direction for 24 hours. The deity of this zone "Moon" has 16 dimensions, i.e. 16 virtues. All the virtues of moon give happiness, coolness and peace. This is the first nostril of cosmic breath that provides energy passage for all time, day and night. Astrologically this zone is represented by 4th house that is happiness and luxurious life. Proper

DEITIES OF NORTH ZONE		
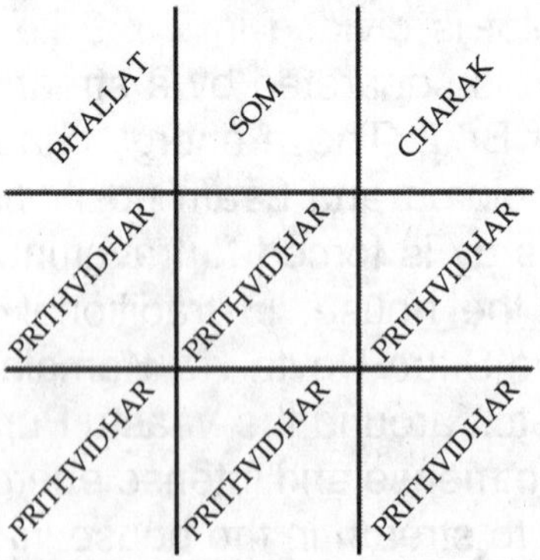 BHALLAT	SOM	CHARAK
PRITHVIDHAR	PRITHVIDHAR	PRITHVIDHAR
PRITHVIDHAR	PRITHVIDHAR	PRITHVIDHAR

Figure 11.10

and ample streaming from north zone represents good condition to house. It is a source direction of Ida-Chandra Naadi, hence this direction represents *Stree-Tatwa* or ladies. So this zone gives softness, micro skills, arts, serviceability and passivity. Any troublesome person if aligned in this zone with head to east, will cool down; his biorhythm will get adjusted, leading to a useful nature. Pearls, crystals, depression, light, silver and water are the cosmic equations related to this zone. When light travels from north to south, then it travels along the electromagnetic- flux. In traditional language it is called "Pranik energy and organic energy are in the positive confluence, which is the highest bliss in cosmic equations". To improve the quality and order of any space it is a simple trick to open the north zone, so that light travels from north to south, i.e. from source to sink. A forward mandalacar streaming is possible if north energy streams in the spaces because north energy has potential virtue of water. Indian philosophy quotes that deity of north is a virgin lady with peacock as her vehicle. Her name is Uma, who fulfils all wishes, wills and ambitions. Sutra as follows:

उदीच्यां पातु कौमारी॥ कौमारी शिखीवाहना॥ इच्छा शक्तिउमा कुमारी॥

In Yogshastra it says that "One who gets related to the Ida-Naadi he experiences peace, prosperity and progress. Hence, in a way purpose of Vaastu Shastra is to align everybody with north streams, so that everybody forms a cosmic relation with Ida-Naadi. In industries, research and development, cabins of main important people, and all creative intellectual work should be in this zone, a very clean space with ample light and white marble flooring should be present in this zone. A small water body/fountain with crystals and mirrors reinforce the organic streams. Use of silver and pearls enhance the quality of moon streams.

h. Northeast zone:- Here lies the head of Vaastu Purusha. In Yogshastra it is said "sun element is in naval zone with face turned downwards (AdhoMukh). Moon element lies in head with face outwards (BahirMukh). Deity Shiva in chakraform lies above head, beyond the moon." Same reference could be traced in Ratnadhyay. In naval portion Ruby is placed. In head zone, i.e. in north-east zone pearls are placed. Whereas, in the outer sky of northeast zone, crystals representing "Shiva" are placed. In a way by this ritual, a real passage of energy from northeast to southwest is cleared by this process. The deity of this zone is "Rikta" or a "Space". This is the zone where the helix of cosmic energy begins and moves in a mandalacar path. Water element of north can be equated to prosperity but water element of northeast is equated to the Teertha or divine waters of

> In case of Kirloskar pneumatics, the factory shed had too many obstructions on the path of the energy. Many mezanines of multiple levels created a mess in the streaming, light and Ventilation. Though the shed had a north-south length, the effective area never represented any order and discipline. The entire north zone was raised loaded and shabby so though the north was open, energy was absent. In such cases just cleansing the paths of energy creates a virtue in the space, which leads to progress and prosperity. Some mezanines were dismantled to clear the flow of energy. Some old machines were removed from the working zone. Huge openings to north and east started pouring the organic and pranik energy. Transparent sheets in north and east zone gave an positive aura to the whole space. Just regulating the energy stream played a fantastic role in the creativity, production and discipline.

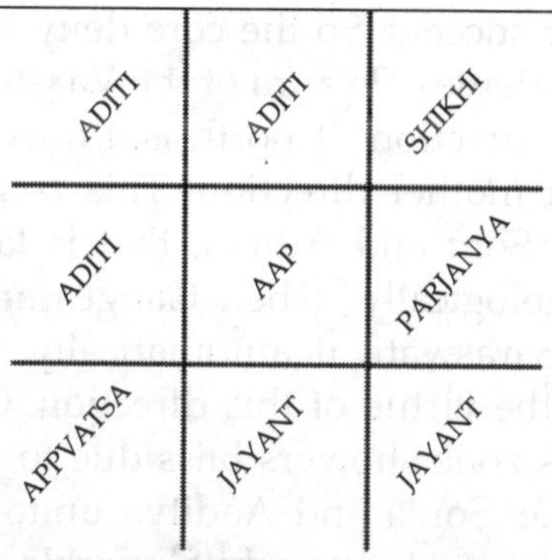

ADITI	ADITI	SHIKHI
ADITI	AAP	PARJANYA
APPVATSA	JAYANT	JAYANT

DEITIES OF NORTHEAST ZONE

Figure 11.11

Ganges. Water in north is perishable but grace of northeast water is everlasting. A core deity being Aap, i.e. Jal-Tatwa, is surrounded by Aditi, Diti, Shikhi, Parjanya Jayant and Aap Vatsa as Aavaran devta. Aditi and Diti represents sunlight. Shikhi represent the *Jyoti* form of fire or Agni. Parjanya represents natural bliss of water from sky. Jayant

> The Mumbai International Chhatrapti Shivaji airport has a unique shape which assures peace in the present period of turbulence. It has a crescent lunar shape that opens out to north. Water represents streaming and movement. When water is channelised it leads to a discipline, order and forward movement. This airport is the busiest airport of India and highest movement is observed in this Vaastu. If at all any violence happens (violence means fire) due to tranquilising water shape, this violence will subside and will not lead to any huge losses. In addition if 9 flags get erected to the south zone and a huge waterbody is done in the northern zone/entrance zone, then this Vaastu format assures peace, prosperity and progress.

is the deity of success. So the core deity is surrounded by all divine sub-deities. So aura of the Vaastu is related to the virtue of this direction. If north is a queen direction then northeast is a mother direction. This zone represents the confluence of Som and Aditya, that is Jaivik and Pranik energy. Mythologically, when Ganges and Jamuna meet the form of Saraswati, it automatically starts emanating light. This is the virtue of this direction. One can say that quality of this zone showers bliss due to which mind and intelligence, i.e. Soma and Aaditya unite together. Space, voids, depression, light, white marble, water element, pearls, crystals and silver adds virtue to this direction. In industries, one can align chairman and directors, cabins, research and development, arts and prayers to this zone. A simple treatment, like transparent sheets in this zone, works well in the energetics of Vaastu. Some additional borewells excite the earth energy. Use of white marble blesses the virtue and order to light. Silver and pearls accelerate the moon streams. In a way the assembly of water, light silver, pearls, depressions and crystals represent the each deity of northeast-square, which hardly happens in other cases. In practical case studies, a huge machine kept in this zone had spoiled the quality of the entire factory. In another case study, blue containers in this zone had spoiled the character

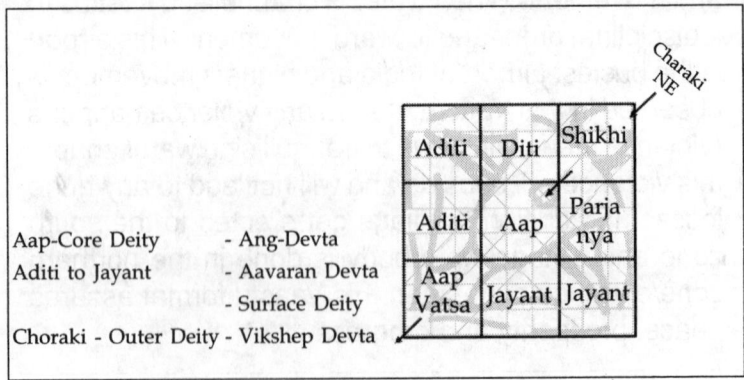

Figure 11.12

of entire zone in Vaastu. Pearls are placed in Aap-division to give strength to the Ang-devta. Shivas crystals are placed between Shikhi and Charki, to keep Charki away from the main square.

> Simple remedies for industries, in which one need not do any change inside the factories is of prime importance, as it doesn't indulge in the day-to-day routine. a) Provide nine borewells in a lunar geometry to the north and northeast zone. b) Provide nine mounts in landscape to the south zone. c) Plant nine Christmas trees/Almond trees to the south zone d) Erect nine golden/yellow colour flags to south zone. e) Provide pyramidal structures to south zone. f) Keep all garbage load, steel racks to south zone g) Bury lead/steel metal to south zone h) Paint yellow colour to south sloping roofs. i) Provide transparent sheets to the north slope. j) Provide circular white marble pieces to north zone. k) Provide lunar shape waterbodies to north zone and do the finishing in white marble. l) Shift the big plants of north zone to southside m) If any machines, clarifyers or huge cylinders are in north zone then at least paint them in white or silver colour.

12

Cosmic Remedies

a. North Zone:- Following are the severe faults of north zone:

(*Mahadosh*)
1. If north is closed.
2. If north is loaded.
3. If north is less.
4. If north zone has toilets/septik tank.
5. If there is hill to north.
6. If north site margin is less
7. If north zone has a staircase
8. If north zone has any heat treatment plant.
9. If north is loaded due to heavy machinery.
10. If there are no windows to north.

Due to this blockage at source zone, rest of the factory becomes a big void. When north energy and east energy streams simultaneously then the resultant vector force creates a mandalacar pattern and path of energy. This is termed as a positive confluence of Pranik and Jaivik energy. If mandalacar streaming does not happen then aspirations of directions remain thirsty of Chi, leading to the loss of aura of core and surface deities. Automatically the outer element Vikshep deity becomes active and disturbs the entire energetics of industry.

These are the steps to be followed to avoid this:
1) Create a deep depression in north zone so that earth energy gets transformed in the organic streams, leading to north as a strong source zone.
2) Place 108 pearls each in 9 holes formed in a crescent shape.

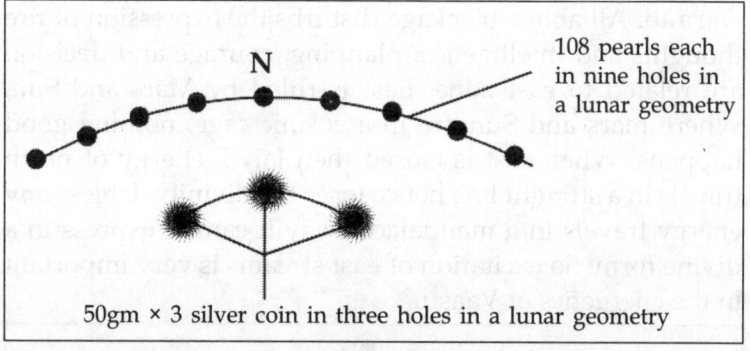

Figure 12

50gm x 3 silver coins in three holes in a lunar geometry. This will enhance the quality of moon streams. Earth energy will get a Sanskara of ritual and muhurat by placing these pearls and silver.

3) Provide a fountain with depression, lunar shape, with white marble flooring and crystals kept in water. This assembly of crystals water and white marble gives a divine virtue to rays of light.
4) Use of mirrors in above assembly will enhance the organic streams.

b. East Zone - These are severe faults of east direction (Mahadosh) –
1. If east is closed.
2. If toilet is to east zone.
3. If east is loaded.
4. If staircase is to east.

5. If east side has no windows.
6. If there is a hill to east.
7. If site margin to east is less.
8. If there is a water body to east.
9. If road hits from east.

East zone represents the fire with a flame, fire with warmth. All above blockage disturbs the expression of fire thoughts and intelligence, planning, courage and decision are related to east zone. East is ruled by Mars and Sun. Where mars and Sun are in a cosmic cage, nothing good happens. When east is closed then Jaivik energy of north travels in a straight line hence loses the divinity. Unless any energy travels in a mandalacar way it cannot express in a divine form. So excitation of east streams is very important in the energetics of Vaastu.

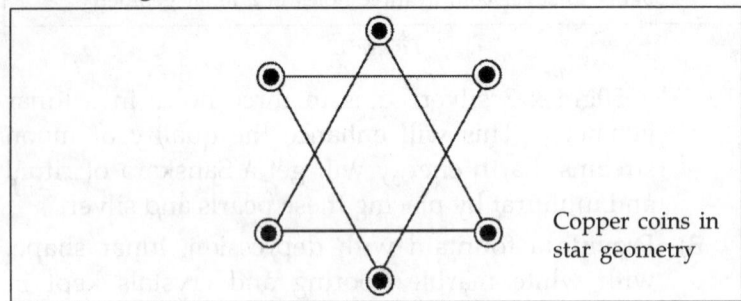

Copper coins in star geometry

Figure 12.1

a) Provide depression to east zone, which in traditional language is called "Poorva- Plava- mahi" that becomes "Vruddhikari", meaning "earth with slope to east leads to progress."
b) Plant a banyan tree in east zone.
c) Place red coral in the inner zones to accelerate the mars effect of east. Place crystals in the outer sky to keep away the Vikshep deity, viz. "Indra- skandha".
d) Provide deodar wooden panelling to east surface, inside the property.

e) Bury copper coins at the tips of star geometry say 50gm each x 6 apex points of star geometry.
f) Provide large windows and transparent sheets to east slopes and side.
g) Do not provide toilets, heavy machinery, lofts, mezzanine floors in east zone.

c. **West zone:-** Following are the severe faults of west direction (Mahadosh):
1. If West is more
2. If there is void/duct to west.
3. If there is slope to west.
4. If West had many windows.
5. If there is a valley to west.
6. If site margin to west is more.
7. If kitchen is to west.
8. If there is terrace to west.
9. If there is a depression and a water body to west.
10. It road hits from west.
11. If shape of the building is "C" opening to west.

If additionally east is faulty then it is a dangerous condition. West is zone of a Saturn so it is a sinking zone. To hold the pranik energy of east, west should be high, heavy and less as regards site margin. Saturn represents contraction andreduction. West zones represent partners, court matters and strength to withstand the shocks. A powerful west supports the order of pranik energy of east. Financial recovery and popularity of product is dependent on west zone.

a) Do not provide roof slopes to west or at least maintain the equislope condition to the east-west axis.
b) Do not provide large windows and transparent sheets to west zone.
c) Plant a Peepal tree to west zone and surround it by a small platform

d) Bury or place the 7 nails of lead metal to west central zone in outer margin. In feng shui west is equated to the metal element. Lead being heavy in weight and being a metal with qualities of Saturn, it gives remarkable results. Nailing the metal is like a "Kilak" in traditional language, keeps the outer deity *Jambuk*, a Vikshep devta, away from the inner circles.

e) Bury or hit the 7 bronze rods in (4+3) ascending order, inside the space in the central west zone. Again bronze being metal enhances the west and since nailed holds the position of Varuna, Asur and Jambuk.

f) Provide blue glass, blue flooring to the west zones. Blue being of a Saturn quality, reduces the streaming of west.

g) Provide pyramidal umbrellas or ceiling to substructures. Pyramids are a good medium to control the west streams.

h) Provide Aluminium metal panelling to west walls.

i) Refill the wells or borewells by stones and concrete without any second thought.

J) Bury 7 blue Sapphires to west zone inside the factory.

k) Construct the C-shaped building opening to east and north.

d. South Zone- Following are the severe faults of south direction (Mahadosh):

1. If south is sloping.
2. If south is more
3. If south is more streaming.
4. If roof slopes to south.
5. If water bodies are to south.
6. If depression and borewells are to south.
7. If site margin is more to south.

8. It south has more windows.
9. It there is terrace to south.
10. If road hits from south.
11. If shape of the building is "C" opening to south.

In addition if north has a fault then the condition becomes serious. South is a sink zone of Jaivik energy and is a main negative direction, with scorching sun in south for tropical countries and with warming sun in south to Europe, China, etc. This climatic variation changes the treatment to south in feng shui and Vaastu at apparent level. feng shui considers "south" with fire element and Vaastu considers "south" with Mars and Capricorn. It is the architectural environmental demand due to which treatment of "south" changes in Europe, Asia and China not due to feng- shui and Vaastu.

Since Vaastu acts like a two-streams theory, directions have fixed characters as regards source and sink. Whereas feng shui acts like a No-stream theory, all directions are classified on the element basis. Vaastu speaks in terms of aura, and deity, whereas feng shui speaks in terms of aspirations and elements. Ultimately both have a common basic principle *that the energy should flow in a mandalacar way so that it reaches to every corner and place.*

a) Do not provide roof slopes to "south". If roof slopes to south then form a curtain to protect the roof from scorching sun. Provide high ventilation and light from north and east sides.

b) If plot is sloping to "south" at first place try to find the new place. If not then provide the shape of building that opens to north or east. Provide the entire roof slope to north or east. Provide a towering pyramidal structure to southwest zone.

c) If building has a C-shape opening to south then break the central zone, at least open the roof in this zone.

Amid the "future and the present" their lies a form and a space. If form has dynamic symmetry and space has no voids then the future is brighter than the present. If form has no order and spaces have dark shades of voids then the future is dreadful and present is in danger. Vaastu gives a compatible form to the nature and refills the voids by energy to transform them in the spaces. In the oriental tradition this sense of direction and presence of time are clubbed into a single connotation "dik-Kal" the dik means direction defines the quality of Kal, i.e. time. "Time space one continuum" filled by "quantum energy" define the existence, is the basis of oriental philosophy. Whenever north gets blocked, it reduces the spaces and the form gets disturbed. Whenever south gets excited, it disturbs the form and voids gets activated. The massacre of 9/11 has the same background. There were two towers, north tower being higher than south tower, it created obstruction in the energy streaming. South/southwest/southeast zone to the adjoining part of the two towers of WTC had a deep coastal depression and excitation of Pingala/Sun streams of south/southwest/west, which leads to death, destruction, defamation, discontinuity and deletion. The entire north-south axis was disturbed when the cosmic north got disturbed and polluted, and the disaster happened.

Provide a slope to north and a towering pyramidal roof.

Construct a stone wall with towering height to "south" end, so that it bridges the gap that forms the "C".

Provide a lunar-shaped huge water body to north end with white marbles, Pearls, Crystals and fountains.

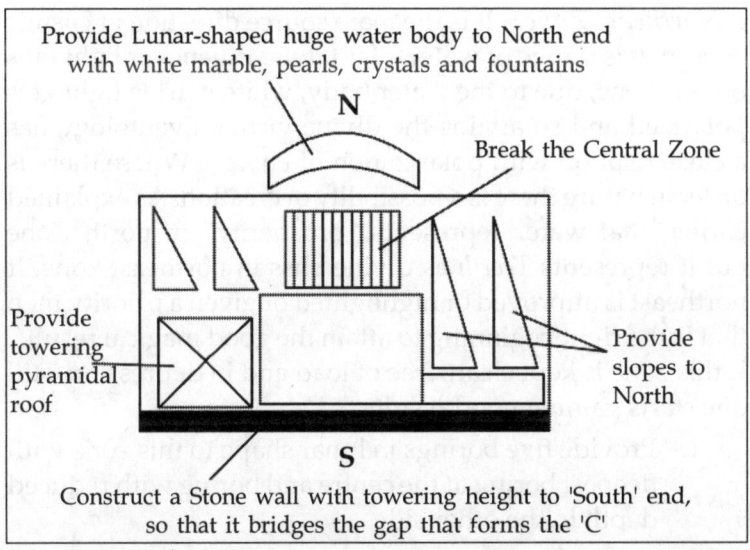

Figure 12.2

d) Provide yellow glass to south side windows to arrest the white light. Yellow represents Pruthvi-Tatwa. Whereas white represents Jal-Tatwa, that cools down the cosmic fire of "south", whereas earth elements make the fire of virtue "Warmth".

e) Use Audumber plants to "south" zone to absorb the negative currents.

f) Use pyramidal umbrella roofs to south zone to absorb the negative Pingala streams.

g) Bury 9 Cats eye stones inside and 9 blue Sapphires in the outside zone of building to control the Gandhrva, Yam and Grahkshat along with Vikat of outer spaces.

h) Hit 9 nails of lead metal inside and outside to control the core, surface and outer deities.

e. Northeast Zone :- It is the main source direction of cosmic energy. It is a zone of water — Jal-tatwa. Whenever light falls on this zone, due to the water body, white marble light gets polarized and so attains the divine virtue. Eventology has a close relation with polarization of energy. Where there is order in nature there is a possibility of creation. As explained earlier, that water represents "prosperity" in north Zone but it represents *Teerth* as divine bliss in northeast zone. If northeast is improved or highlighted or given a priority then that is the right beginning to attain the good magical results. If this zone is kept clean, free of load and in depression, still one starts gaining good results.

1. Provide five borings in lunar shape to this zone with deepest boring at the centre and boring with reduced depth to the other side.

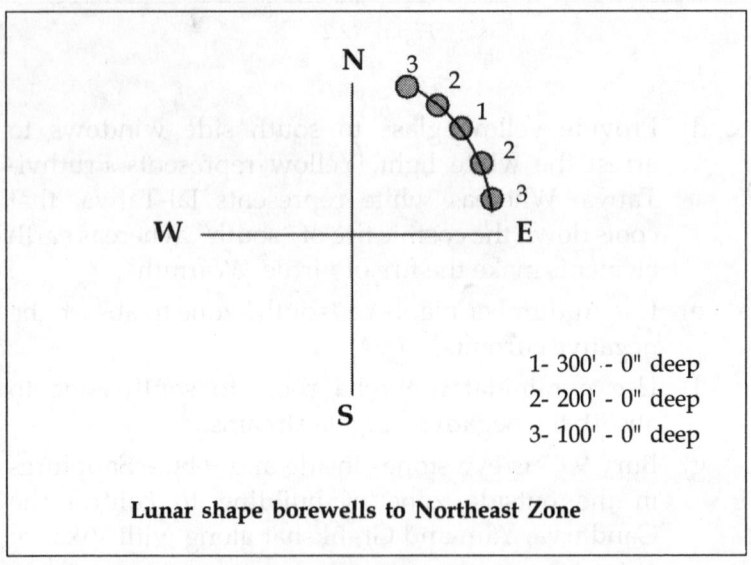

Lunar shape borewells to Northeast Zone

Figure 12.3

2. Provide lunar-shape water body and with depression use white marble for entire flooring of this zone. Place 3 crystals at 8 places in lunar form. Also, bury 35gm Silver at three places

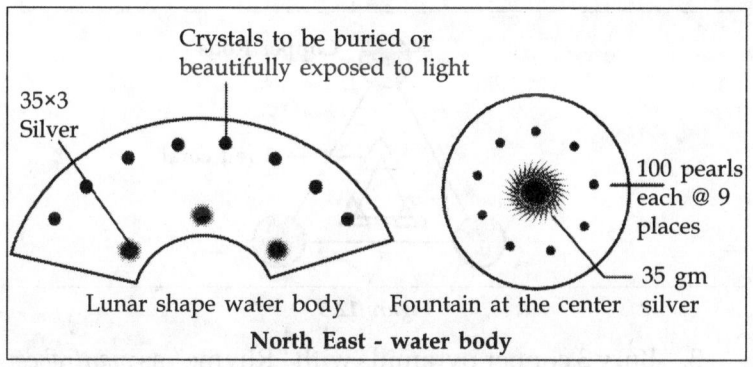

Figure 12.4

3. Provide 20% roof of this side with transparent sheets to get the feel that "the light is getting poured from the corner".
4. If possible keep the chairman's cabin to this zone.
5. In R.C.C. slab provides an opening then seal it with hard glass so the light enters from NE corners and streams like water in the spaces.
6. Provide white or silver colour to entire NE zone so that light travels easily, reflects softly and gets polarised properly.

f. Southeast Direction:- This being the zone of Mars, fire and Venus, southeast represents strength, power, imagination, leadership and ambition. Anything that needs strength, such activity should be arranged in this zone. All generators, inverters, boilers, heat treatment, exothermic process and the start of the process should be in this zone. A small hillock, raised ground, raised plinth gives good results. Any red article is not permitted in this zone.

1. Provide a mango tree in this zone with surrounding platform.
2. Bury copper rods with triangular geometry and bury 3 red corals at the centre of this triangle.

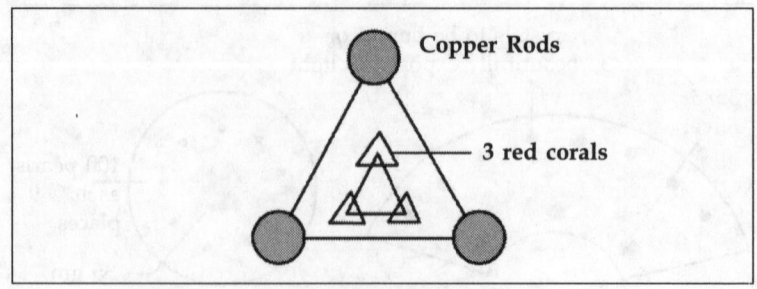

Figure 12.5

3. Bury 3 copper pyramids with "Rhyme" as *mantrabeej* (a seed of primordial sound) with a proper rituals. Place 3 red corals below each pyramid.

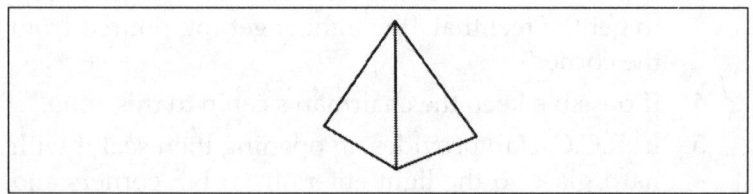

Figure 12.6

4. Construct a substructure as the labour - huts, garages and godown in this zone
5. Do not provide any water elements in this zone.

f. Southwest direction:- This is a main sink direction where negative confluence of organic and pranik stream disturbs the energetics of the zone. To make a balance of this disturbance, a solid earth element is the need of this zone. Earth load is a multidimensional element which can absorb the Pingala sun streams, which can cool down the effects of thermal variation. It provides the stability, fertility and prosperity.

1. Plant 4 Audumber plants in this zone and provide a surrounding yellow stone platform.
2. Bury 4 lead metal pyramids, in this zone with square geometry.

3. Bury 4 Copper pyramids with "Gam" as mantrabeej (a seed of primordial sound) with a proper ritual. Place 4 yellow sapphires below each pyramid. Use square geometry to square pyramids.

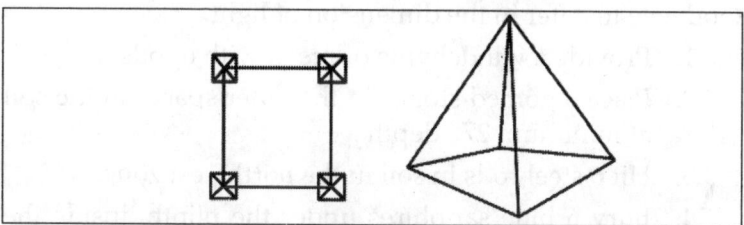

Figure 12.7

4. Provide five vertical rods with golden yellow flags
5. Provide pyramidal substructure in this zone.
6. Always keep a load of stores in this zone.
7. Never provide any borewell in this zone.

h. Northwest Direction:- Keep this zone clean and colourful. This is the zone for finished goods, so ultimate profit is related to this zone. As orders and delivery of finished

---

The success story of Mr. H. R. Gaikwad, the chairperson of Bharat Vikas Group, is interesting. He is a good follower of the principles of Vaastu. He removed the asymmetric zones of his house and relocated the house with "L" shape that spread out to the NE zone. Borewell, sleeping zone, kitchen, windows every possible element is relocated in the house. In office the entrance correction by pyramidal canopy, metal treatment, Ratnadhyaya was done. His cabin has north-south length with proportion of the golden ration. In cabin, light flux is only form N and E zones. Mr. Gaikwad faces north with table top of white marble and to the left in SW corner load of lead pyramid curtails the negative energy. The progress of Mr. Gaikwad and graph of rise in the market is quite vertical and ascending.

products and equipment depends on the virtue of this zone. A nice garden with small fountains can energise the environment. Use of chymes and bells give a virtue to the wind and transcends it in the sound. A rhythmic sound has tendency to enter in the dimension of light.

1. Provide a windchyme of metal with 6 rods.
2. Place 6 gomed stones in the outer spaces in the soil at minimum 27" depth.
3. Hit 6 steel rods in soil in the northwest zone.
4. Bury 6 blue sapphires under the plinth, inside the premises of factory.
5. Keep the segment reserved for finished goods and entertainment anddelivery counters.

In a big industrial set up, if 2/3 of the structures are planned in a way to follow the Vaastu tenets, then the virtue of these spaces will take care of many anomalies in the surroundings. If all important jobs, like research and development, accounts and sales, main chairman's, director's cabin are kept in this zone, then these leaders can change the future of that industry. All such structures, should have either of the four shapes which have proved their excellence. a) C opening to east is called as the Aaditya-Choola. This structure leads to discipline in working, vitality in the research and honesty in the behavior. b) C opening to north is called as the Uttar-Choola. This structure leads to prosperity and abundance in general creativity in the development and fame in the market. c) L opening to north east is called as Dakshin-Pashchim-Dvishala. This structure leads to effortless gain, unique position in the market and monopoly in the product. d) Towering pyramidal roof to south and west alongwith sloping roof to north and east, can be named as Shivlingakuti which is a perfect cosmic form.

13

FORMS OF SACRED GEOMETRY

a. Cylindrical forms :- For a uniaxial structure, this works out to be an ideal form. Due to its cylindrical barrel shape, axial streaming of energy may happen but a virtuous streaming, where "SKY" takes part to improve the quality of each element may not happen. A straight line planning with E-W length will have many additional problems due to projection of major surfaces to a scorching sun. Such a structure has equal shapes to north-south direction. In eventology, energy being a positive energy, it plays a long-term and slow role. Whereas positive energy being a reactive energy has an immediate exploding element leading to devastating effects. Roof slope to north will add positive virtue. Roof slope to "south" will not allow this virtue to get represented on the screen of events.

b. Lean-to-roof:- Many times during the expansions, one tempts to add only to one side by "lean to roof" addition. If this extension is to the sink direction, i.e. to west and south then entire energetics and streaming goes wrong. In case studies, I have seen that such extension have hit further progress and has given great losses leading to liquidation. Hence it is necessary to make the master plan, along with the sequence of construction. In many cases the form and zone are correct but the sequence of construction has gone wrong. This fault has to repay bad compensation. I have to analyse this in many case studies. As the traditional Vaastu Shastra says that sequence has to be from

SE to S to SW to W to NW to N to NE to E

If this sequence is strictly followed then one never gets any difficulty in such Vaastu at any stage of construction there is no blockage of source zone, due to which a free streaming energy is available for all activities. *Shivsutra* says that

चिति: स्वतंत्रा: विश्वहेतुसिद्धी:"

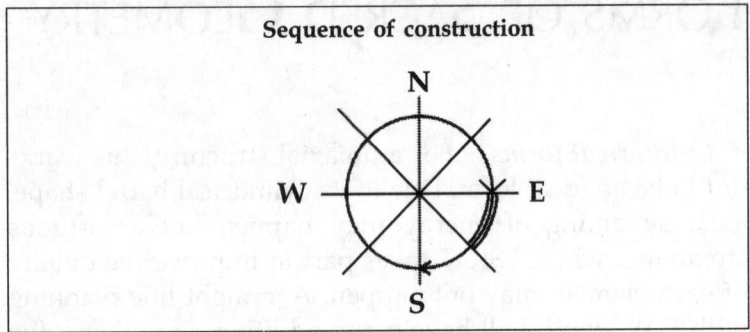

Figure 13

A free streaming energy has a strength and purpose to fulfil the wishes of the entire world. That's why the first roof of construction is erected in southeast zone, which is called *prathameshtika* (the first right thing done). "The deity here is "Nanda", which represents the first day of the month called Pratipada.

A proper excitation of zones as said in a sequence of construction, automatically formulate the Chakra forms,

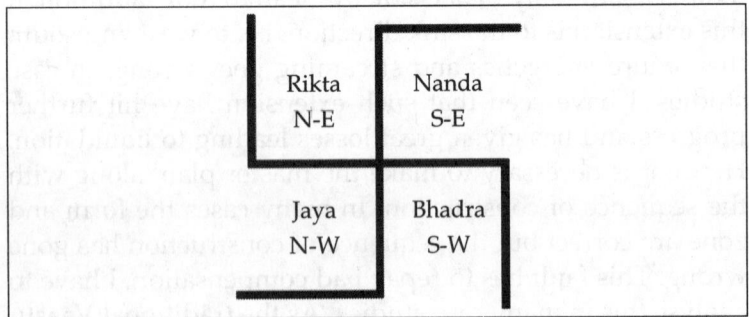

Figure 13.1

that leads to mandalacar streaming of energy. Such a form automatically rejuvenates the Prana to all aspirations, which in turn contribute peace, prosperity and progress to the spaces.

c. Lantern effects in ceiling: - For better participation of sky element, it is necessary to provide some lantern effects in ceiling or some transparent sheet in between. A stagnation of energy will not happen due to this provision. Even a linear speed of energy may reduce leading to a better time–space equation. Circular lantern will effect a better circulation of energy.

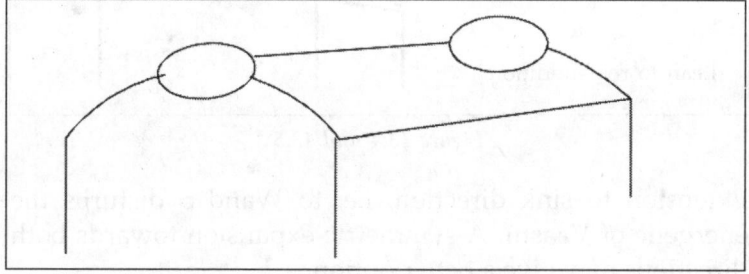

Figure 13.2

Deep pyramidal lanterns at periodic intervals to reduce the straight expression of energy and to improve the participation of sky elements.

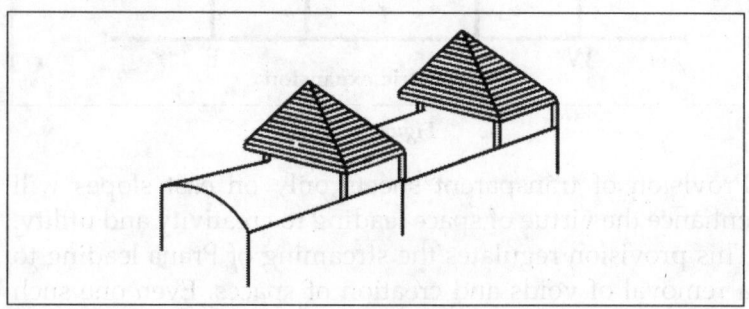

Figure 13.3

Transparent sheets at periodic intervals improve the participation of sky element.

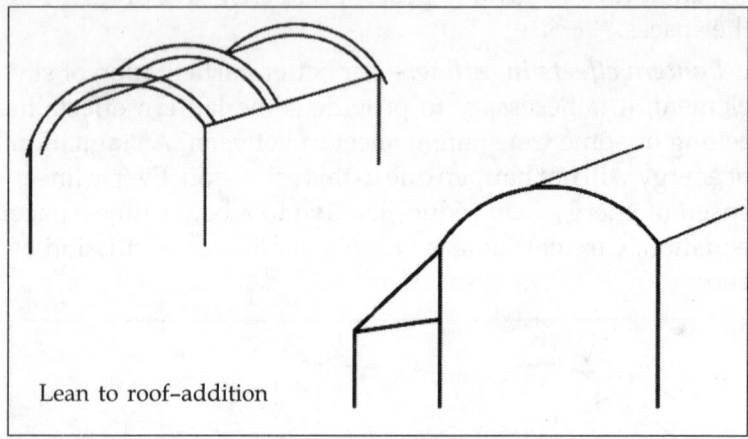

Lean to roof–addition

Figure 13.4 and 13.5

Extension to sink direction, i.e. to W and S disturbs the energetic of Vaastu. A symmetric expansion towards both directions may give a better option.

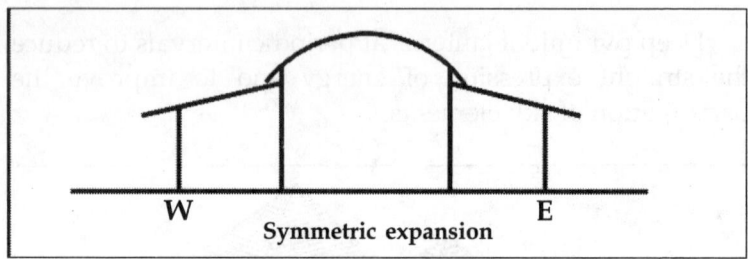

Symmetric expansion

Figure 13.6

Provision of transparent sheets only on east slopes will enhance the virtue of space leading to creativity and utility. This provision regulates the streaming of Prana leading to a removal of voids and creation of spaces. Even one such simple treatment has given magical results.

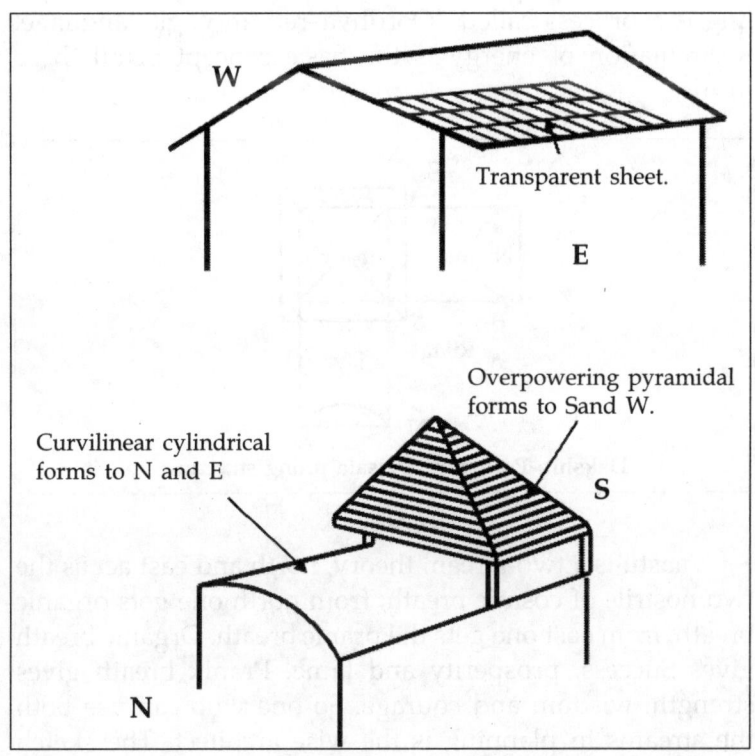

Figure 13.7

d. Ideal forms that lower the source zones and raising the sink zones is the key to Vaastu. In terms of forms, using female forms, curvatures, light effects, tenderness, spaciousness and water elements to source zones elevates the quality and virtue. Using the male, yang forms powerful, unique pyramids to sink zones, i.e. to south andwest zones, maintains the order and discipline. In a way a right participation of yin and yang leads to a "Tai-chi". As said elsewhere in this book this is a cosmic form called Shivling-Kruti. Ling represents the yang energy, Yoni represents a yin format. A Shivling-Kruti is a divine universal form representing a perfect contribution of yin and yang, leading to a Tai-chi. A proper streaming from north and east and raising the energy high to south and west by pyramid or ling is a process called "Oordhva-ret" in yogic language. Recirculation of energy is the basic concept of all these forms.

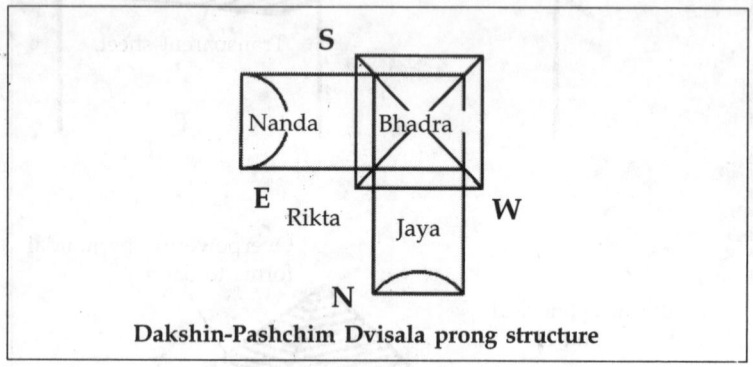

Figure 13.8

Vaastu is a two-stream theory, north and east act as the two nostrils of cosmic breath, from north one gets organic breath, from east one gets the pranic breath. Organic breath gives Success, prosperity and fame. Pranik breath gives strength, wisdom and courage. So one who can use both the streams in planning is the wise architect. The sketch shown is called "Langal"-type construction in traditional language. More specifically it is called "Dakshin-Pashchim Dvishala". In this form if a proper sequence of construction is followed then a deity in order also forms an expression. As it is deity of northeast is "Rikta", i.e. a space which is maintained in this form to suit its character as a "Space". The helix of Vaastu gets completed in a forward direction due to the completeness given by the deity "Rikta" by creation of a space. Moment this logarithmic helix is formed all the deities in Vaastu Purusha Mandala get the prana leading to bliss to all aspirations.

A pyramidal roof to the southwest-zone is a complete yang form, under which the yin-earth element attains the fertility and completeness. A powerful expression of earth element in southwest-zone gives a longevity, continuity and stability to the owner of the house, or factory or premises. Creativity, expansion and bliss of Northeast can flower if the earth element of southwest has a perfect expression.

As explained elsewhere in this book, the *Uttar-Choola* pattern is the only answer for constructing on the earth with slopes to south and north raised. In such a case, cosmic

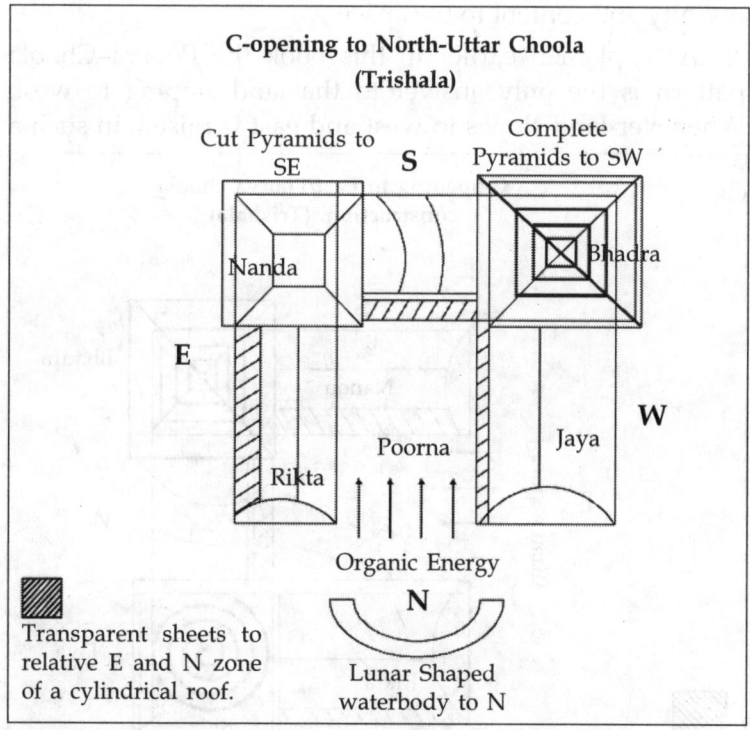

Figure 13.9

fire becomes intense and entire stream character of water element gets vanished. Due to non-streaming of energy, prana does not reach all deities of 81 grid Vaastu Purusha Mandala and the aspiration does not flourish, leading to failure of structure Vaastu. When a form C- opening north is used, then such a form generates and gives acceleration to the organic stream and to the streaming character of water element. A total blockage to the "south", cut pyramid to southeast and regular pyramid to southwest controls the intensity of cosmic fire. Provision of transparent sheets to proper zone leads to the streaming of pranik and organic streams. A lunar-shaped water body, with white marble flooring, pearls, crystals and silver embedded in the mortar below, accelerates the Chandra Naadi Streams to bless the divinity and content to the space.

As explained earlier in this book the Poorva–Choola pattern is the only answer to the land sloping to west. Whenever land slopes to west and east is raised, in such a

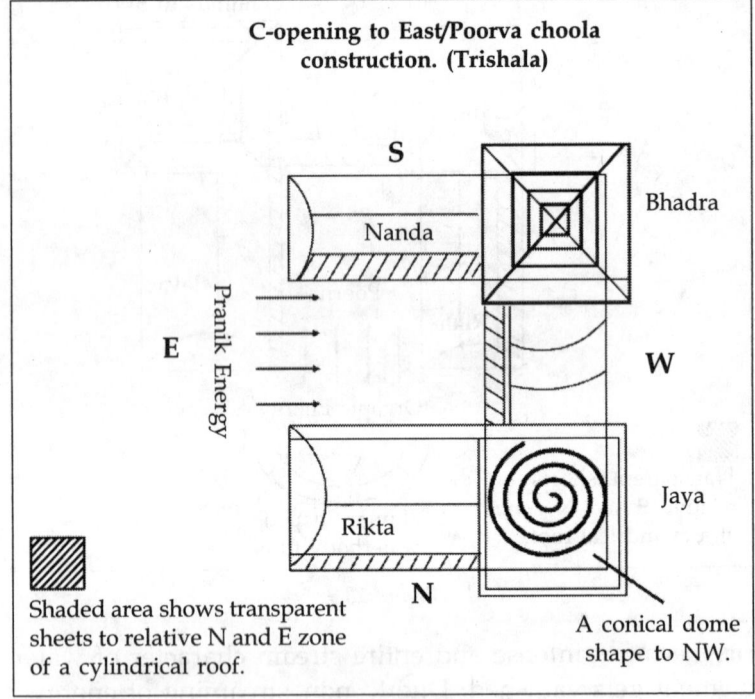

Figure 13.10

case the bliss and sanskara of Aditya gets lost leading to a wrong expression of fire or Agni-Tatwa. Expression of fire in east is a flame, jyoti, but expression of fire in southeast is explosion.

Where land slopes to west then outer deities, viz. Jambuk, the vikshep devta becomes active, leading to death of Mahendra and Satya of east zone; asur/varuna deities of west work for the vikshep devta "Jambuk" leading to the death of Angdevta "Mitra". This excessive cosmic wind creates the Catrina and Rita in the energetics of Vaastu, leading to the total failure of Vaastu Purusha Mandala, this turmoil turns the *charkha* of events in an anticlockwise direction leading to deaths, destruction and discontinuity. The structure C-opening to east, generates and gives acceleration to pranik energy leading to a warmth and light of Aditya. A regular cylindrical shape to southeast promotes the energy to a mandalacar form. A regular pyramid to southwest stabilizes the intense wind. A confined west controls the power of cosmic wind.

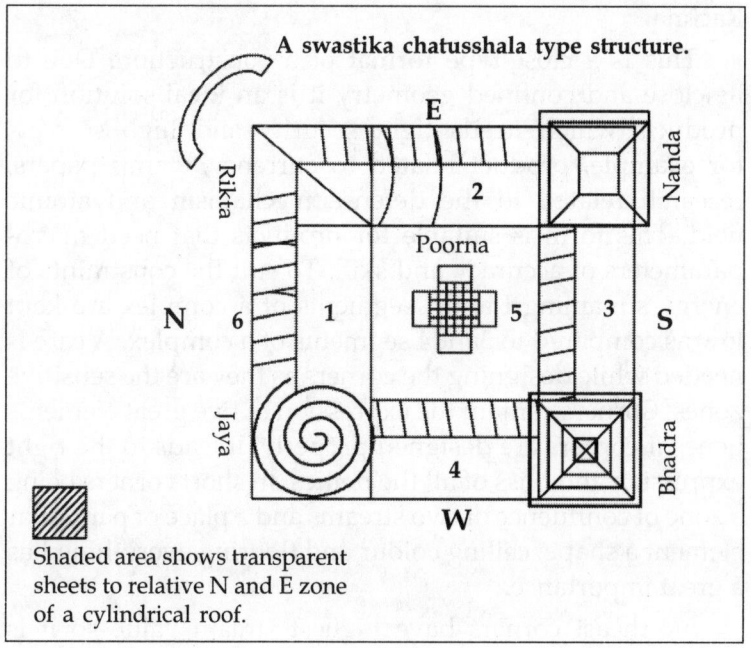

Shaded area shows transparent sheets to relative N and E zone of a cylindrical roof.

Figure 13.11

1. Sloping, leaning and lowest—point to northeast corner.
2. A cut pyramidal roof to southeast—a second highest point in Vaastu.
3. A regular pyramidal roof to southwest—a highest point in Vaastu.
4. A dome type conical structure to northwest.
5. Fountain and water body to Brahmasthan.
6. Shaded area shows transparent sheets to relative north andeast zone of cylindrical roof.
7. Lunar-shaped water body to northeast corner.

Lunar-shaped conical structure over northwest transforms the wind expression in the sound form, leading to a divine primordial sound wave. That's how the Poorva-Choola pattern works and creates wonders in the Vaastu Rachna.

This is a close-type format of a construction. Due to its close and confined geometry it is an ideal solution for products which needs tight security and high secrecy, for example, product related to currency, stamp papers, research related to the defense mechanism and atomic field. This form is suitable for products that need micro-parameters of accuracy and skill. To suit the constraints of energy streaming I andII segments of a complex are kept low as compared to 3and4 segments of a complex. A care is needed while designing the corners as they are the sensitive zones. Corners contain the expression of five great elements hence if corners are designed properly, it leads to the right expression and bliss of all the deities. In short corners being a zone of confluence of two streams and a place of particular element a shape, ceiling colour and flooring everything has a great importance.

Northeast corners have highest stream value so it is maintained low and is connected to its elements, viz. water, Jal-Tatwa, by a lunar-shaped water body with depression, fountain, white marble, pearls, crystals and silver. Southeast corners contributes strength, warmth and accuracy which are expressions of fire — Agni-Tatwa, which is covered with a cut pyramid to maintain the quality of cosmic fire. Cut pyramid maintains the warmth quality and does not allow it to explode and spread. Southwest corners are designed for the earth elements — Pruthvi-Tatwa, which gives stability, prosperity and fertility. A regular pyramid has power to control, to curtail and to hold the entire negative currents of south and west. Its flowering nature indicates the healthy yang elements that can embrace nourish and create the healthy element under its aura.

Southeast zone being basically a zone of yang element, i.e. fire if it is provided with red colour, fire accelerates and leads to explosion or ash. A conical dome to northwest zone gives higher dimension to wind. It transforms the wind in to sound, which has immense positive divine virtue. In central zone a water body with sacred geometry enhances the quality of Brahmasthan, this water body promotes the mandalacar stream of energy. This is the zone where the cosmic romance of yin and yang creates a rhythm and synchronicity. In traditional language it is called as Shiv-Shakti-Sangam, confluence of actual deity and its power together.

14

SOFTWARE INDUSTRY AND CALL CENTRES

This industry has been the cause for many lifestyle-related health problems in the society. Basically, because of erratic working hours , which are against the natural cosmic order and a solar cycle. The work involved is mechanical, repetitive, stagnant and highly competitive, though salaries are quite impressive as compared to the other disciplines of engineering that becomes an attraction for such jobs.. The working hours are to suit the overseas assignment, but natural order and solar cycle gets disturbed which has an immediate effect on rhythms of hormones. Automatically this deficiency leads to change in the cycles of breath leading to excitation of wrong Naadi. When wrong Naadi gets excited it has a direct effect on Prana and Apana Vaayu. Yogshastra mentions about a wrong relation to sun and diseases related to mind. Sun does not mean the sun outside but it is a comprehensive terminology to the elements of sun which lie in a seed form in the body. Sun in the human body is represented by Intellect, Pita, Agni, head, qualities inherited from father, Suvarna content (Gold) in the body, and activities related to the excitation by the sun. Rather one can say that entire right side of a body is part of the sun. So this wrong routine, wrong eating and wrong cycles of nature have deep-rooted effect on body, mind and intellect. So these technocrats need a perfect support of Vaastu principles to get a biorhythm in life..

Wisdom of Eighteen Maharishis as expressed in traditional science has given thought to the problems of modern man. To resolve these problems Rishis have given comprehensive thought to Vaastu, Yoga, Astrology, Music and Ayurveda. In their time, Nature and Vaayu-mandal (orbit of wind) was free of any pollution, so that was the time when hardly anybody was in need of these oriental sciences. Now due to media, cell phone, televisions and advertisement along with industrial pollution, entire Vaayu-mandal is polluted. This pollution has direct effect on brain secretion and levels of hormones in body. It is easy to control Catrina and Rita which are in the outer world, but it is very much difficult to regain the order, discipline and virtue in this polluted orbit of wind (Vaayu-mandal). Unless one uses some breathing technique, some Divine forms in Vaastu, some tranquilizing tunes of music, some silent colours to take mind on silent mode, some herbal medicine to remove the toxins, one is bound to remain diseased at one of the levels, i.e. Body (physical phenomenal). Mind (Psychological) and intellect (spiritual).

a. People with the Sun sign Aries, Leo and Sagittarius — 15 Apr to 15 May, 15 Aug to 15 Sep, 15 Dec to 15 Jan.

These signs represent fire element, Agni-Tatwa. Such people should try to regulate the fire element by following techniques.

1. Sit in east zones facing north. Avoid seating in southeast zones. East zone is the zone where fire is represents a flame (= Jyoti). North is a source direction of organic streams and direction of Jal-Tatwa. (=Water elements).

2. Use blue and white colours for walls, computer screens, tables and chairs; if possible provide white marble to table top.

Prefer to remove shoes and put your bare foot on a white marble tile to cool down the Optic nerves.
3. Concentrate on a gold spot for 2/3 minutes after each 2 hours gap and take long deep ujjayee breaths.
4. Keep one or two crystals (Sphatik) at hand and feel the transparency, softness and lustre while working or while thinking.
5. Use sandalwood paste as a Bach therapy for exciting the moon rhythms. Nose is an ultimate sensitive organ which connects the outer spaces to brain through routes to the hypothalamus.
6. *Jap* of mantra beej "Rhim" with prolonged sounding and resounding activates and transforms the voids into spaces, at deeper levels of being.
7. If mind gets irritation or hyper excitation, try silver water therapy on Monday and Friday in early morning hours.

If mind becomes nervous, pessimistic then try gold water therapy on Sunday, Tuesday and Thursday in early morning hours.

b. People with the sun signs Taurus, Virgo and Capricorn — born in 15 May to 15 June, 15 Sep to 15 Oct, 15 Jan to 15 Feb.

These signs represent the earth elements. For better rhythm these people need more yang energy. To activate the sun element they should try the following techniques.
1. Sit in the west zone and face east direction with large air column open to east. Activation of Pranik energy activates the yang–charka in the body. Bury a small Ruby below the Zone of chair or below the table top.
2. Use pleasing light pink colour to computer screen. If possible use furniture made of deodar or pinewood with fresh polish. If possible use the sandals made of cane grass and wood, of organic material.

3. Concentrate on a red spot for 2/3 minutes after each 2 hours gap and do Bhasrika breathing for 5 to 7 strokes after each 4 hours.
4. Hold the Rakta chandan beeds in hand. Feel the fragrance and cosmic power of the herb in the working period.
5. Use the pure camphor as the Bach therapy to excite the yang rhythms in the body.
6. Jap of mantra beej "Eiim" with prolonged intuitive sounding and resounding transforms the inertia into profound energy.
7. Herbs like Hirda-Behda, if chewed after food, will reduce the vaat tendency and will activate the hunger. A pranayam called "Agnisaar" will be helpful to maintain the balance of digestion.

c. People with the sun signs- Gemini, Libra and Aquarius – born in 15 June to 15 July; 15 Oct to 15 Nov; 15 Feb to 15 Mar.

They represent the wind elements (=Vaayu-Tatwa). Their basic constitution being of Vaayu-Tatwa, if Vaayu-Tatwa remains balanced they enjoy the life. To activate and regulate the Vaayu-Tatwa they should try the following technique.

1. Sit in southwest zone and face the northeast direction, with large air columns free to north and east direction. They have a high thinking power, so if they face the Northeast, give a tranquillity and peace. Use white, light blue or silver colour on computer screen and surrounding furniture.
2. If possible, make egg-shaped solid silver balls and just keep in hand or surroundings while working. Hang a wind chime of 7 silver tubes to relative west zone, along with some blue crystals.
3. Concentrate on blue sky with a continuous easy look, without strain, at deeper depths. This will give immediate relaxation.

4. A gentle breathing with technique of Naadi-shodhan or a technique of Vipasana will be of great help.
5. Drink the water in silver pot. If possible take a small dose of "silver water" on Monday, Wednesday and Friday in the early morning hour.
6. Jap of mantra beej (Gam| |Shrim| |) with prolonged intuitive sounding and resounding energises the wind elements in the body.
7. Herbs like *Ashvagandha* and *shatavari* – combination will give vigour and balance of IQ and EQ.

d. People with the sun signs Cancer, Scorpio and Pisces – born in 15 July to 15 Aug. 15 Nov to 15 Dec, 15 Mar to 15 Apr.

They represent the water elements (Jal-Tatwa). These people have hyper mind and face a high-low tide. To regularize the water elements they should try the following techniques.

1. Sit in north zone and face north while working. In this case, south should be firm, confined and should use white marble top to table. Place 3 pearls each at 9 points in lunar shape below the table top of marble. Use white and silver colour on computer screen with predominant water elements in pictures. Keep silver articles like plates, flowers pots in the vicinity with surface studded by pearls.
2. Use pyramidal roof to cabin by using deodar or pine wood. Deodar pyramids have divine power to shower a peace and bliss.
3. Concentrate on a crystal *Shree-Yantra* in the flame of pure ghee. Use the mantra beej Shrissm with prolonged intuitive sounding and resounding to reduce the effects of low tide.
4. Use white aromatic flowers or similar scents in surrounding to energise the brain.

5. A regular intake of Chyavanprash and seasonally Gulkand will give better concentration and power. To activate the sun elements, a regular exercise of Bhasrika will be of great help.
6. While sleeping use the organic axis, head to the south and legs to the north. The problems of people involved in software field and call centres are odd and complicated.

Now let us discuss the ideal forms for the buildings, where these psycho-somatic problems can be resolved due to a right expression of five great elements and a correct form that connects the divine cosmic energy to the spaces.

e. Nine Remedies

1. Natural light: Light should travel from source to sink. This is the natural path for photons to give a forward travels and effect. Natural light has a white colour, so it has a virtue of Jal-Tatwa (water elements), which gives streaming in a mandalacar way, so it is known as divine. White light can be considered as an ultimate expression of vibrations of particle as it has order, content, discipline and pattern. When a positive confluence of five great elements happens it gets constituted in the Sunrays, a white ray. Whenever light travels from east to west then it energises the entire space by pranic energy. Since it starts from east, it carries the grace of Mahendra Ravi, Aditya, Satya and Aayana, which represents a warm expression of fire (Agni-Tatwa) Since this light sets in west, it contributes prana (chi) to the Mitra (the central Anga-Devta) of west zone. So the entire west zone remains related to the central Brahma zone and not to the Vikshep deity, viz. Jambook.

In the fundamental concept of Vaastu Purusha Mandala, one should know that when Anga-Devta (deity in the central zone) becomes powerful then energetics of Vaastu remain balanced, e.g. Pruthividhara of N, Aap of NE, Aryama of E, Savitra of SE, Vivswan of S, Indra of SW, Mitra of west and Rudra of NE are powerful then entire Vaastu Purusha Mandala gets governed by central Brahma. The traditional definition of Brahma is "That which remains in state of progress and active vibration". All remedies of Vaastu Shastra have a unique reference to create the mandalacar streaming of energy so that all central zones deities get a continuous streaming of prana whenever light travels from N to S, it makes a positive confluence with organic streams. In traditional language it is a *Chit Vilas* (a *sangam* of Jeeva and prana) astrologically it can be explained as "Gaj-Kesari yoga" a confluence of Jupiter and moon. It can be explained as "gold with divine aroma". If this one thing is attained in Vaastu then it eradicates most of the evils. So provide more opening to N and E; provide larger site margins to N and E; provide reflecting surfaces to N and E; provide water bodies; white marble to N; provide depressions and slopes to N and E, provide opening in ceiling to N and E.

2. *Central breathing zones*

In industrial structures continuous long shades and halls are necessary for various continuous processes. In this case one has to divide these spaces and create effectivity of Vaastu Purusha Mandala in comfortable zones. So such cuts and discontinuities in halls are necessary to redistribute the energy, to re-energise the prana and chi and to create effective mandalacar streaming. A very long corridor creates a straight line streaming of energy. Feng shui believes that evil energy travels in a straight line with impact force and stroke, whereas divine energy travels in a mandalacar way with turns, curves and bliss. Normally the ratio of length to breadth should not be more than 2:1 ratio; means if length is 100'-0" then width should be at least 50'-0" so that energy redistribution becomes possible. In many cases this is not possible due to practical needs. In such situations, use of transparent sheets, forms, pyramids and colours play an important role to turn the path of energy, to create the curvatures in a path and to redistribute the energy. This parameter breaks the excessive speed of energy without any stroke, friction and blockage. Funicular cones, helical structure, wind chimes exhaust fans and roof shapes have powerful strength to redistribute the cosmic energy.

When central zones are kept free for the sky light, the deity Brahma gets the energy in that zone and connects the element of Anga-devta to formulate a new grid of Vaastu

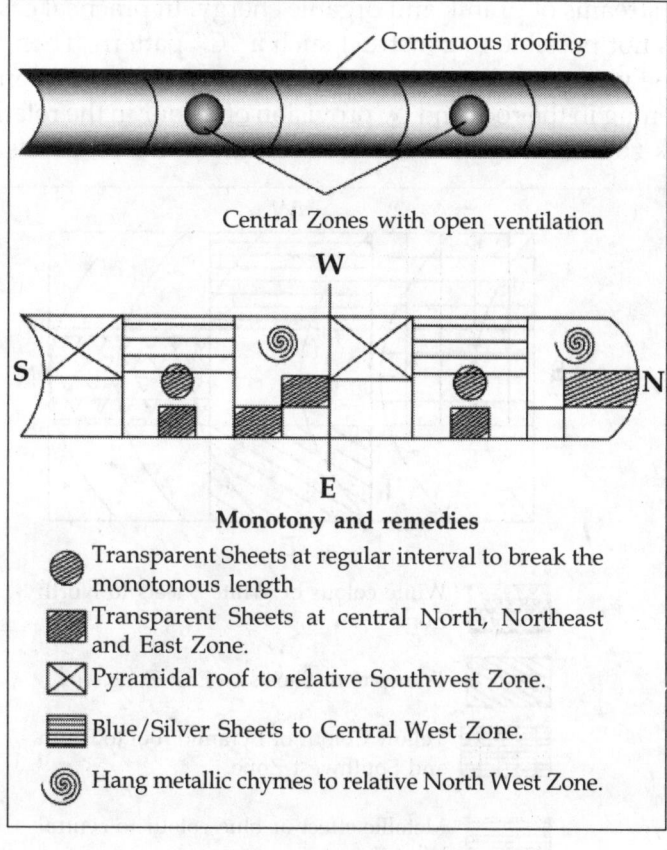

Figure 14

Purusha Mandala. That's how ratio proportion and zones are automatically redistributed.

Such treatment can break the excessive length and can create more interactive spaces with helical streaming of energy.

3. "C- forms" opening to North and East

As already explained previously in this book, Poorva-Choola and *Uttar-Choola* are the divine patterns to regulate the streams of pranik and organic energy. In practical cases, it is not possible to construct such a "C" pattern. Then the same virtue can be attained in the factories by provision of opening in the roof and by provision of colour in the relative sink zones of roof. Provision of colours in the relative sink

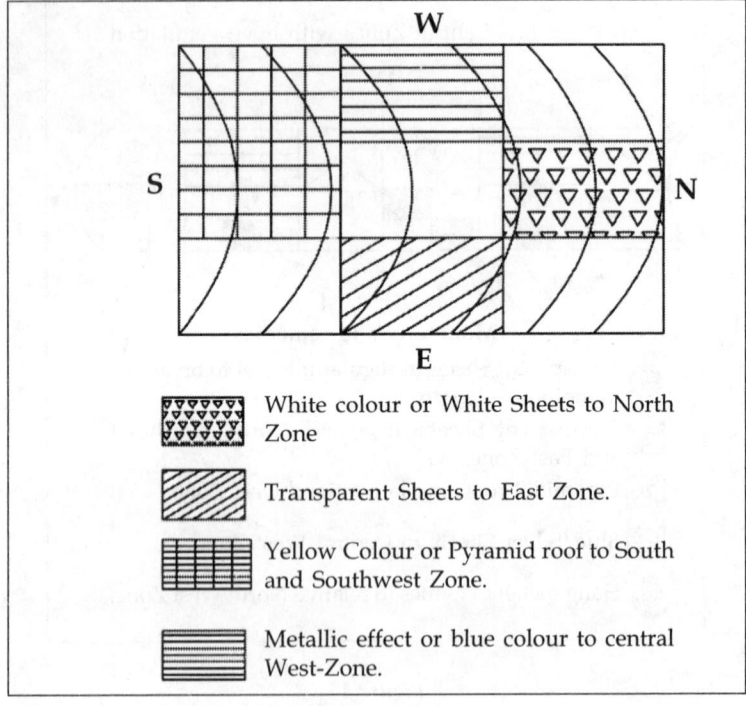

Figure 14.1

and source is given at roof level, automatically five great elements get energy by correct redistribution of energy.

Transparent sheets to east will enforce the light energy to travel from east to west. So the grace of deities Mahendra, Aditya, Satya and Aryama gets distributed in the entire space.

Yellow colour to south and southwest zone or pyramidal roof to south and southwest zone will stabilize the earth element in proper way.

Metallic effects to west add a virtue of venus and mercury to this zone. Whereas the blue colour regulate the qualities of deity Pawan. Treatment of white transparent sheets to north is right justice to water elements. That's how colour, forms, elements and transparent sheets can create an effect and virtue similar to the Poorva-Choola type, C-opening to east structures.

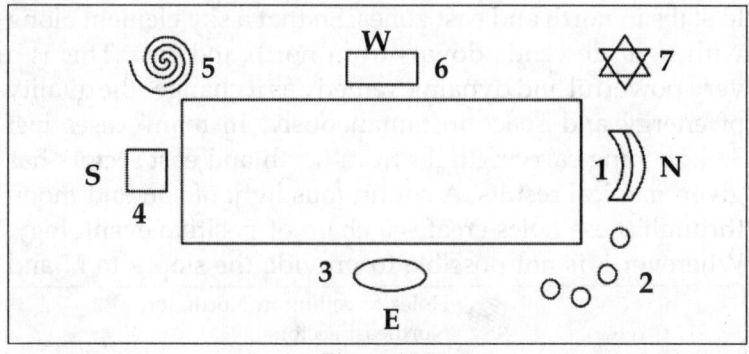

Figure 14.2

Reflection of the roof at the plinth level by adjustment of loads, high-lows colour and landscaping will naturally support the helical streaming of energy.

1. Provide lunar-shaped water body to N with white marble, pearls, crystals and silver.
2. Dig 4 holes in a lunar shape to NE zone with effect as borewells and depressions.
3. Take an oval-shaped depression to east and plant Durva (=medicinal Green grass) and Green bamboo.

4. Raise the south level. Plant Audumbar and Golden, Yellow Bamboo.
5. Provide a heavy landscape in rocks to southwest.
6. Provide pyramidal roofs metal structure to west zone.
7. Provide a bell tower to northwest in metal frame.

All above mentioned remedies are externally placed without disturbing the internal layout. These remedies will keep the Vikshep deities (i.e. outer deities) away from the factory, so that possibility of disturbance gets reduced.

4. Terraces to North and East

To accelerate the organic and pranic streams, terraces to N and E directly open the spaces to sky elements. In basic planning, if this provision is done then that will be the ideal way of working. If not then one can create the core cut holes to slabs in north and east zones. So that a sky element along with light descends downs from north and east. This is a very powerful and dynamic remedy as it changes the quality of energy and space instantaneously. In many cases just 3/4 opening carrying light from north and east sectors has given magical results. A continuous light of son and moon through these holes creates a chain of positive eventology. Wherever it is not possible to provide the slopes to N and

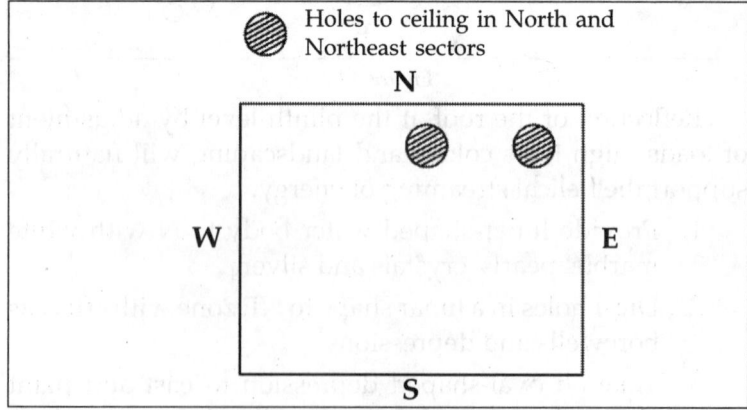

Figure 14.3

E, at all such places opening the ceiling directly to sun and moon plays wonders.

5. Golden ratio (1:1.5)

It is called as a sacred cut, or a divine proportion. A proportion of a logarithmic spiral that represents a positive energy or a divine force is in golden ratio. Anything has a golden ratio, works and lasts long. It is the path that has least friction and impedance as regards streaming of energy. In feng shui, it is a customary to follow the sacred cuts and ratios. In Vaastu this proportion is taken care of through the use of "arm length" of the house owner and its multi-proportions to decide the floor height, windows and doors. Vaastu has given a deeper thought in this serious subject of cosmic befitting of divine energy and personal aura.

So it is beneficial to use doors and windows in golden ratio. It is also better to use golden ratio while planning the sizes of the cabins. It is necessary to place 1 along E-W axis and 1.5 along N-S length; then it has a cosmic order. As organic streams travel in this space for a longer time, seeds of positive events floating in an aura form lie in the organic streams, so these seeds get more time to get flowered in the reality. A secret of eventology is the secret of Vaastu Shastra which lies in N-S length of any unit.

6. Fish ponds and water bodies

A live water in relationship to light is a source of yang energy. Apart from this, feng shui believes more in fishes as they are the best medium to absorb the negative energy. A pair of Arowana fish is considered as a great protector in negative events. I have experienced this myth to come true in two cases.

As per Vaastu principles, such fish bowls, tanks and fountain in N/NE zone work as booster to the Chandra Naadi Pravah (organic streams). It has a great cooling effect in the field of electronic clutters, radiations and artificial environment. A TRATAK (a continuous eye steering) on such water bodies, reduces the mental tensions and irritations. Use of Silver, Pearls, Crystals and White light along with the water body enhances the quality of Jal-Tatwa (water elements). A better streaming from north and east due to such mediums, creates a better possibility of mandalacar path in the space. If a natural light falls on such water bodies then a real magic happens in the energetics of entire Vaastu. Lotus shapes carved in white marbles and

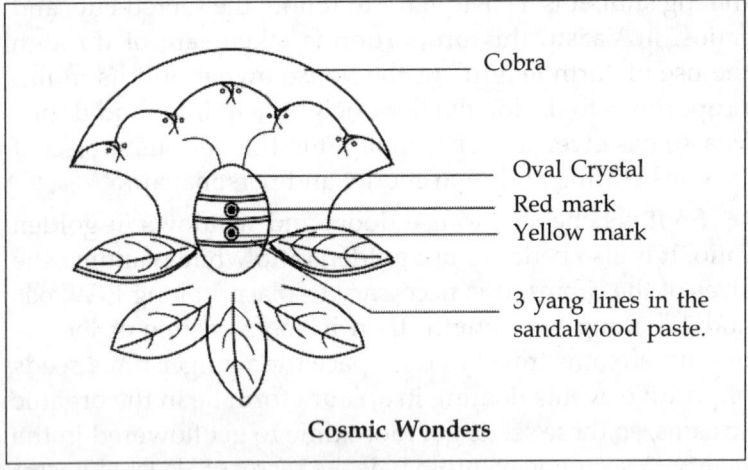

Figure 14.4

oval-shaped Sphatiks placed on these lotus with the focus of natural light will play wonders. Three yang lines on Crystals with Red dot as Tilak, Yellow dot as supporter to Tilak, has a great power to transcend the quality of space.

Forms and Symbols is a mystic subject; they contain the key of cosmic energy. Various *yantras*, sacred geometrics, mantra beejas pour a positive sequence. Use of specific materials and forms has a great cosmic and architectural meaning. Indian tradition is a unique technique that connects the reality and cosmic dreams to such yantras, tantras and symbols. Chakra, Padma, Swastika, Mandala, bells, conches are quite popular symbols. They act as carriers of traditional mystics grace and explode like a great continuity and relationship to the grace of forefathers.

Indian tradition believes in metaphysical existence. The grace and cosmic order descends through the deities. These deities possess different orbits and levels of existence. Excitations of spaces due to a mandalacar formation of energy automatically create the positive form of deities in zones and directions. These are divine forms with sacred, ordered geometry, which share its divine grace to human beings. This is a vast subject and could create a new book an eventology.

7. Use of pyramidal ceilings:- Pyramids control the energy and curtail the negative vibration of energy. It acts like a sink; it contracts so its nature is like a Saturn. It adds to the qualities of Pruthvi-Tatwa so it is close to Mars. As in feng shui, "fire is considered as supporter to earth element, as it creates ash," similarly pyramids act like a supporter to earth element. A definition says that a "Pyramid" means "a cosmic fire at center". It is a silent form of fire so it gives warmth. Astrologically south zones act as own place of Saturn and place of excitation to Mars. Pyramid has a same quality and relationship to Saturn and Mars.

a) If sink directions are cut or extended in the building then, use pyramidal ceiling in this zone. Since pyramid sinks, curtails and cuts, the effects of extensions get controlled. In case of cuts, pyramids by way of its square forms, contribute the effects of completeness to the aspiration.

b) Use the pyramids to SW and W zones to control the negative stream. In this case a thought to elements plays wonders, which has a direct relation to feng shui. Feng shui is an eight-elements theory where one finds the relation of element and directions. Vaastu speaks of forms and colour in correlation to the five great elements. Use White metallic pyramids to west zone. Astrologically, west is represented by mercury, Saturn and Venus. So use of bronze or aluminium or White metals takes care of planetary classification. In feng shui, metal is equated to west zone. Use of stainless steel foils to create pyramidal form will give good results. Use wooden pyramids to control the Southeast and South zones. It is preferable to use pine or deodar wood as the bio-rhythmic cycle of this wood matched to that of the human being. Wood being an organic material, Vaastu Shastra has high regards for it as a material of construction. Use Jaisalmer Yellow stone slabs to form the pyramids of SW-zones. Yellow colour and stone both promote the quality of earth elements. The more you use the earth element to SW means better prosperity, stability and fertility in the space.

8. Colour: Use White or faint-blue colour to the ceiling, so that ceiling acts as the source of sky and wind elements. Eight directions, elements, space and their virtue is the base of colour treatment. A firmer south, passive west, active east and streaming north makes the space creative. So stone cladding to south, metal panelling to west, wooden panelling to east and white colour to north is an ideal formation. To break the monotony, a 10% intermingling effects of elements give a yin-yang benefit, i.e. Tai-chi effects.

Generally north and east should have a White colour or Silver finish. Southeast should not have any range of red colour. South and southwest should have either of black, brown and yellow. North and northwest should have a metallic, blue and pink. These colours are based on the elemental and planetary classification of directions.

9. Table tops: It is a good and healthy thing to use wood as the base material for a table top. Normally one concentrates on reading or on computer screen so organic soft wood gives a cooling effect. To reduce the effect of focusing on the subject, use a crescent-shaped, lunar-shaped top, with use of White marble and a small inlay of Silver metal. Place 9 pearls each at 9 spots in lunar shape on wooden base and fit a White marble top on this wooden platform. It is preferable to face north and then to east as a second option. A logic behind this facing lies on the fact that a body is divided in yin and yang, i.e. moon and sun elements (with left as moon and right as sun). So when one faces north, left part representing moon matches to the northwest, which is a moon-zone. A right part faces to northeast which represents light in Vaastu Purusha Mandala. When one faces east, left part of face matches the natural moon streams, right part of face matches the natural sun streams or fire elements. While seating, it is necessary to have a firmer south or west, i.e. there should be a strong support of wall or element. For instance, while facing north, south wall should have a *Bhoum Yantra* or Stone Copper cladding. While facing east, west should have at least a partition of metal element.

15

ASTRO VAASTU CONCEPTS
(Period of Red Alert)

Saint Dnyaneshwar quotes that:

उपजे ते नाशे, नाशे ते पुनरपि दिसे। हे घटिकायंत्र जैसे चालुले गा।

That which takes birth, ends. That which ends, again rises. It is like a play of time and event. Rather nothing perish but enter in a new form.

A concept of logarithmic helix of energy, C- relationship and Omkar –Pranav are based on this longevity, divinity and continuity. Every form has some purpose and some mechanics. If purpose and mechanics is changed, one needs a new form. Market, industrial product, pattern of economy and pace of time all are dynamic factors. They are dependent on each other and are independently related to many other things. Scope of correlation is unlimited and vast. With this understanding of a floating vessel in sea, wind, rocks and coast one should design a form of Vaastu to retaliate all shocks and to absorb all the known and unknown strokes. The form of Vaastu should merge in the natural expression of five great elements.

This Astro Vaastu concept is a dynamic understanding of time and space. If a proper compromise and adjustment is done by use of matter and energy to protect the Vaastu then in the difficult period a Vaastu survives. A knowledge of weak zones in Vaastu and position of planets in the sky gives the proper schemes to readjust the rhythm of Vaastu. Following aspects are helpful to know the procedure of Astro Vaastu concept.

Classification of directions depends on many factors.

a. Five Great Elements

Directions	Elements
North Northeast	Water
East Southeast	Fire
South Southwest	Earth
West Northwest	Earth and sky.

b. Source and Sink

North- Source direction of organic streams.	South – Sink direction of Organic streams.
East – Source direction of Pranik streams.	West – Sink direction of Pranik streams.

c. Axis

North-South is a Jaivik	- organic axis.
East- West is a Pranik	-solar axis.
Northeast-Southwest is a Water	- earth axis.
Northwest- Southeast is a Wind	- fire axis.

d. Planets

Directions	Planets
North Northeast	moon and Jupiter
East Southeast	mars, Venus Jupiter
South Southwest	Jupiter Ketu Saturn Rahu.
West Northwest	moon, Rahu Saturn.

e. Cycles of Nature

A concept of chakra in feng shui is helpful to understand the virtues of planets and 5 great elements. The chakra of creation, chakra of mitigation and a chakra of destruction are the three wonderful concepts in feng shui. If a secret of this chakra is understood then one can use various elements and medium effectively as a tool to rectify the faculty in Vaastu. A logic and concept of these cycles and of form school are of practical importance to know the effectiveness of elements and expressions of energy.

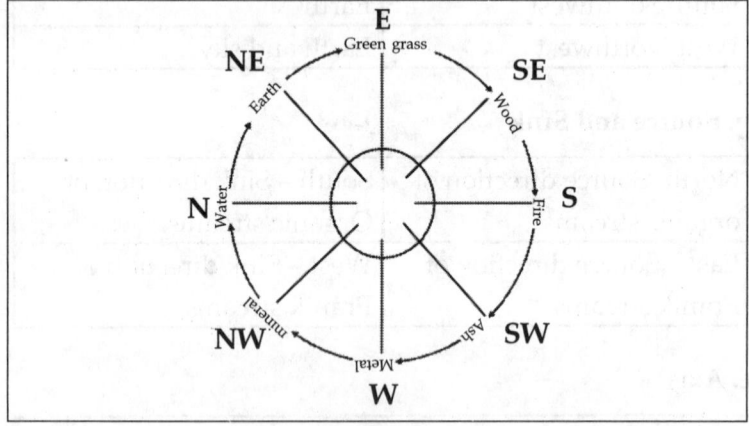

Figure 15

f. Theory of Astro Vaastu

It is wonderful to know that every element and aspiration is directly related to the central zone. In Vaastu this zone is called "Brahma, where sky and earth meet together to create the fortune of the resident. In this zone excitation of "yang energy" is achieved by placing an "eye or seed of sun", i.e. Ruby, which gives the aura and vibration of sun to the space. Invariably, there remains some fault in every structure. Sometimes it may be the fault of high lows and curve counters in Vaastu, i.e. land. At times though everything is well-balanced but a huge towering construction comes to the north and east zones, which blocks the organic and solar streams. At some places new quarry spots create deep depression to relative south and west zones, so that accelerated sun streams create a panic in the whole adjoining area. Due to process of productions, some machines do not match the source zones. Due to exothermic processes high temperatures may disturb the west and north or northeast zones.

All such faults, which create blockage and hindrance to the mandalacar streaming of energy, may create a panic when the position of planets also hits the same directions where the fault lies. It is better to analyze every structure and industrial process with time interval of 5 years, so that a crucial planetary period can be marked. A Vaastu expert can reinforce the Vaastu with some additional remedies for that period, so that wave of negative energy will get distracted, status of industry remains cool and confined. Let us take some events and earth as a mega-Vaastu to understand the sink of zones aspiration, planets, great elements, directions and events.

Astrology and Vaastu are the two sides of a same coin, which get tossed in life as an event. Tracing back and forward will open the eye to see the eventology and future. In general signs and direction are associated as follows.

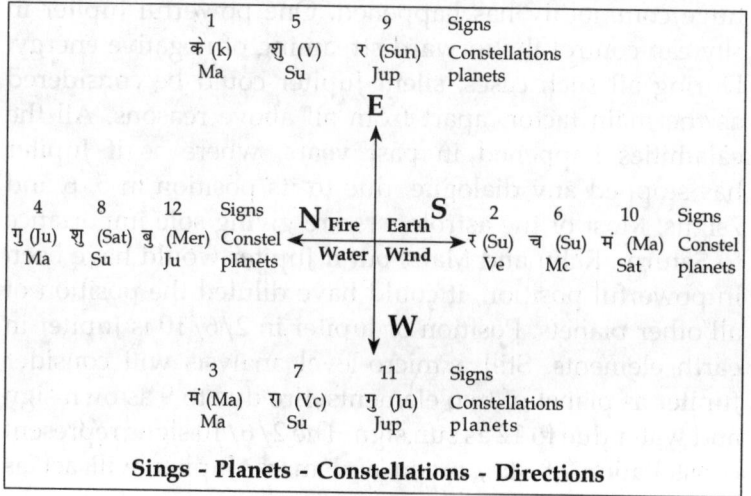

Figure 15.1

With reference to (Figure 15.1) the logic is, if negative confluence happens in 3/7/11 signs then events may happen in west zone, or with effects of wind elements. If negative confluence happens in 1/5/9 signs then event may happen in east zones or with effects of fire elements. If negative confluence of planets happens in 2/6/10 signs then events may happen in south zones or with effect of earth elements.

Sometimes, it is seen that when all planets are in Ketu and Rahu constellation, negative energy reaches the summit; mega events with effects on the history of century do happen when distant planets like Harshal, Neptune and Pluto take part in the negative energy. Negative events, 1, i.e. Aries and 8, i.e. Scorpio, are very important due to their natural negative combination. For example, 1 = Aries representing Mars, sun and fire elements. It contains Ketu constellation which also represents cuts, curtails and fires. Scorpio,own house of mars contains constellation of energy planets Jupiter and Saturn. Scorpio represents 8th house of horoscope where all hidden elements are stored. With this information, let us enter in the discussion of some negative events that have taken away thousands of lives and loss of huge commodity has happened. One powerful Jupiter in sky can control the forward streaming of negative energy. During all such cases, silent Jupiter could be considered as the main factor, apart from all above reasons. All the calamities happened in past years, where as if Jupiter has stopped any dialogue, due to its position in 5, 6 and 7signs. Most of the astrologers are giving sole importance to Saturn, Rahu and Mars, but if Jupiter would have been in powerful position, it could have diluted the position of all other planets. Position of Jupiter in 2/6/10 is Jupiter in earth elements. Still a micro-level analysis will consider Jupiter as planet of two elements, fire due to 9 as own sign and water due to 12 as sun sign. The 2/6/10 signs represent constellation of sun, moon and mars. Jupiter will act as "fire" when it is in sun and mars constellation. Same Jupiter will act as water when in moon constellation. When one considers Jupiter as the deciding factor for events, one has to understand its elemental classification. Whenever the sky is under effects of 1/5/9 then the Jupiter may give effect as fire. Whenever sky is under effect 4/8/12 then the Jupiter may act as water element. In short one should understand that event is more dependent on element than the planets. Base of eventology lies in the excitation of elements, so planets and constellations act as a guideline.

With the all above explanation now let us discuss the practical applicability.

g. River to south

It means that ground slopes are to south, north is high. As per feng shui water on south leads to loss of power fame and energy.

Basically this is a severe fault or "Mahadosh". In any case hardly 5 to 7 years is a survival period if north and east has good conditions, qualities and virtues. South being the main sink direction, effects are intense, definite, direct and severe.

1. Particularly in each month when moon passes through the 9/10/11 signs, Sagittarius, Capricorn and Aquarius, south zone will get activated leading to positive streaming of energy on factory space.
2. Every year when sun passes through 9/10/11 signs, Sagittarius, Capricorn and Aquarius, again south zone will get activated. This period will be a gap of 3/4 months, so for a long period negative cosmic energy will be in force on the factory spaces. Specifically the time of "no moon day" will be very much critical, during which there is a high probability of accidents, lock-outs, labour problems, etc.

3. In a cycle of 24 months when mars travels through 9/10/11 signs again south zone gets activated. If this happens in the months of December, January and February then sun is also in 9/10/11 signs. This period of sun-mars conjunction will definitely create a collapse in the smooth working of a factory.

4. Along with the above combination of planets, if a situation comes when Saturn or Rahu are passing through 4/8/12 signs, then the cosmic north becomes silent and ceases to give organic streams. Saturn shrinks and contracts whereas Rahu fires and pollutes the zone. So north is polluted, along with severe Vaastu fault in "south" then this could be exact period of total failure, destruction and discontinuity. Following horoscopes explain the probable aspect of planets.

In such position of planets, as we see that north is polluted due to Saturn and Rahu, sun, moon, Mars and Ketu activate south, due to this is a most difficult period for north-south axis, i.e. for organic axis. All the factories where lies fault on north-south axis are bound to face some critical problems and bad event.

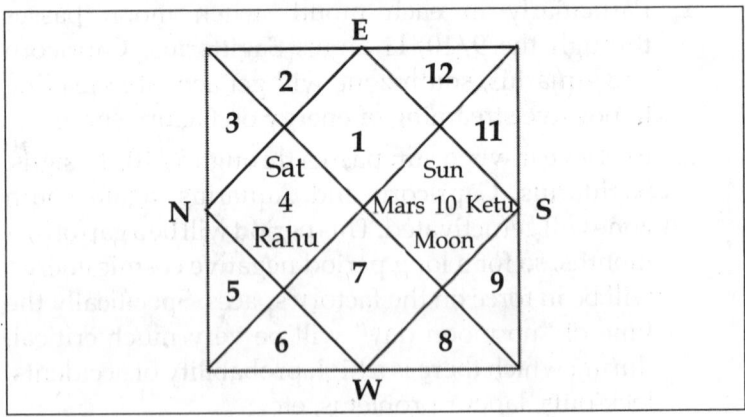

Figure 15.2

Fault on north--south axis: This can be generally explained as the contraction of north and expansion of "south". This situation happens if a) north is high and south is low; b) South has huge water body; c) Factory has North light roof, d) South site margin is a more than north site margin; e) north is loaded due to big machines and light comes from "south"; f) Factory has east-west length. The planetary position as given in this horoscope will definitely create a severe fault in the working of factories with the above mentioned faults.

h. River to west

If some factory has river to west zone, it means that ground is sloping to west, east is high. In such cases, there happens a disagreement in everyday life and working. Particularly partners face confusion and conflict, which leads to malfunctioning in factory. This can be generally explained as the contraction of east and expansion of west. This situation happens when a) East is high and west is low; b) West has huge water body; c) Factory has east-west length; d) West site margin is a more than east site margin; e) East is loaded due to heavy machines and light comes from west.

Along with above faults, even the water to east contributes to a failure. Slopes to east have something good as regards east zone, but this leads to southeast low and northwest high condition. Hence water to east and slopes to east may contribute to total additions to the polluted zones of energy. East represents fire elements, rather in the cyclic emergence of 5 leads to fault in the entire five zones, i.e. east/southeast and "south. In traditional scriptures it is said that fire has ten dimensions. Every movement, action, force represents one dimension of fire. Particularly in industrial structures, where creativity, power, strength and volume are concerned fire element has immense importance.

Now let us find the planetary position when east-west axis has a global problem, which may give worse effects to the structures where E-W axis has severe fault in general when moon enters 6/7/8 signs, it gives strength to positive sinking streams of west zone, i.e. 7 days in each month.

Every year when sun enters 6/7/8 signs, it gives strength to the negative streams of west zone, i.e. around 2 ½ months in every year—i.e. in October end, November and first half of November. Along with above mentioned year by cyclic period, whenever Saturn and Rahu enter the 1st sign, this creates contraction and pollution to Aditya streams of east. This situation comes once in 27 years for 2 ½. Secondary negative results are possible when Saturn and Rahu enter 5th and 9th signs, by way of which they pollute the five elements, leading to bad effects to E-W axis. Following horoscope explains the probable aspects, which may pollute the E-W axis.

In such a position of planets we see that Saturn and Rahu in 1st sign have totally contracted the east zone. Moon and sun in 7th sign have expanded the west zone , Mars in 10th sign has badly affected the Sat-Rahu confluence, by right angle aspect. Planetary positions do not pollute the direction only, but they disturb the balance and equation of five great elements. Hence, while analyzing the Vaastu, it is necessary to give attention to the formation negative waves

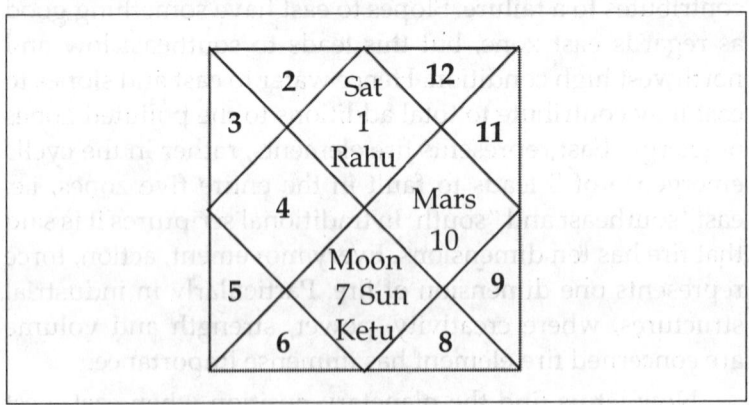

Figure 15.3

in the outer world, through wrong sequence of various planets.

i. Temporary essential remedies

It is wise to understand the dynamics of various forces which happen due to planets and five great elements. Steps to analyse:

a) Find the strength of axes in your factory. For example, if production is related to endothermic action then it has more importance to N -S axis. If product is related to exothermic action then it has more importance to E-W axis.

With reference to above 4 axes, one should classify the product and its alignment with the axis. Products related to ladies are classified to the organic axis. Then clear passaging of energy on this axis is of prime importance. Luxury items and products related to Venus are classified to the wind-fire axis. So toilets and septic tanks to NW, though allowed in general Vaastu will disturb the cycle of energy for this axis.

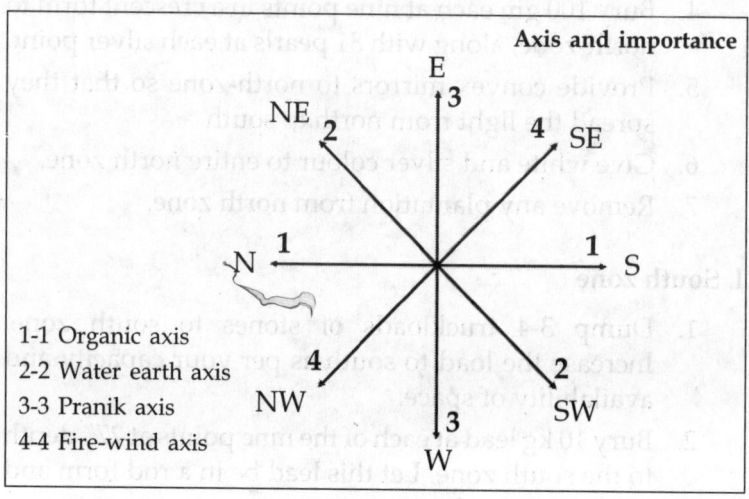

Figure 15.4

In short one should understand the relation of product and the axis, so that more care to improve the particular zone is possible.

Following temporary remedies are helpful to counteract the effect of the confluence of wrong sequence of planets.

j. North zone

1. Provide a deep depression, which may not match the logical mind. In many cases, this depression may create a physical discomfort but choice is yours, weather to digest the cosmic discomfort or to bear temporary physical discomfort.
2. Provide 9 additional holes by borewells, in a lunar shape to the boundary zone of north side. This may be a little costly affair but it will not create physical discomfort.
3. Provide white marble to entire north-zone, so that water element becomes active in the North zone, leading to improvement in the organic streams and Ida-Chandra Naadi-Pravah
4. Bury 100 gm each at nine points in a crescent form to north-zone, along with 81 pearls at each silver point.
5. Provide convex mirrors to north-zone so that they spread the light from north to south.
6. Give white and silver colour to entire north zone.
7. Remove any plantation from north zone.

l. South zone

1. Dump 3-4 truckloads of stones to south zone. Increase the load to south as per your capacity and availability of space.
2. Bury 10 kg lead at each of the nine points at 27" depth to the south zone. Let this lead be in a rod form and place it in a nail pattern.

3. Plant 9 Audumber trees to "south" zone and provide platform form in Yellow Stone.
4. Construct temporary pyramidal roof structures to "south" site margin.
5. Bury 9 each Blue Sapphires at 9 points in the south zone on an auspicious day with proper chanting of Mantra.
6. Provide 9 Yellow flags to south zone with high Steel Pipes near the building zone.
7. Construct towering stone walls to south zone, nearer to the building.

m. East zone

1. Create "C-opening to east" shapes by removal of some structures of east zone.
2. Bury 50 gmX 6 copper Coins at the tips of star geometry at three places in east zone.
3. Remove all plantations from east zone and shift to west zone.
4. Bury big Crystals in a Star shape to east zone with proper time and correct vibration of Mantra as given in *Ratnadhyay*.
5. Do not provide any water body or temple to east zone.
6. Use white marble, wooden panelling, mirrors and crystals to enhance the east zone.
7. Bury 7 red corals in the east zone, inside the building/plinth with right chanting and proper time.

n. West zone

1. Bury 5 kg x 7 lead metals at 7 places in the west zone, on Saturday early morning.
2. Bury 7' long 40 mm steel rods vertically to west zone, near the building.

3. Plant 7 Peepal trees to west zone and provide platform to these trees.
4. Bury seven Bronze rods, 500 gm each, inside the west zone of the plinth.
5. Remove and refill any depression or well or Nala of west zone.
6. Provide 7 towers of metal chimneys to west zone.
7. Bury 7 Blue Sapphire each at 7 points in the west zone outside the plinth area.

16

Hospitals and Nursing Homes

Introduction

Pain, sorrow and hardship are the content of these spaces. Healing, recovering and becoming are the purpose of these spaces. Given a chance, nobody wants to enter these spaces. Specialization, ultra-modern facilities, scientifically advanced techniques, use of computers in operations and huge investments have entirely changed the scenario of this

noble profession and have ended it in a clever business. Patients and users are not against spending some more money but break in the ethical values and reliability have spoiled the main stream of these divine services. Author has given a basic form and layout of one of the famous super-speciality hospital of Aaditya Birla foundations.

Normally 5 types of people representing 3 sets of planets use the space of hospitals. Patients are under the attack of Saturn, Mars and Rahu. Doctors are under the aura of Jupiter, Mercury and Sun. Surgeons are under the influence of Mars, Sun and Venus.

Nurses and operators are under the control of Saturn, Venus and Ketu and trustees are under the influence of Saturn, Jupiter and Sun. So these 5 types of people share this space. The forms discussed in Chapter 12, point 4 are equally applicable for all hospitals. Now various elements of a hospital and their placement could be as follows.

a. North zone: It is a healing zone. ICU should be in north zone with firmer, confined heavy south. Beds should be such that "head to south and legs to north" is maintained. Lights could be arranged on north and east wall to create divinity in the space. Since the character of north is to stream, newly operated patients should not be placed to north zone, for initial period. If firmer south is not possible then place the beds such that "head to east and legs to west" is maintained. If north is closed then at least east should be open to facilitate the pranic streaming. North–south length represents a divine proportion and sacred virtue.

b. Northeast zones: It is the most auspicious and divine area. Do not keep any storage, godowns, load or toilets to this zone. It is preferable to have maximum openness, voids and spaces, so that positive energy gets created in the zone. A waiting lounge for relatives could be placed in this zone, since they are in prayers and in chanting moods. OPD and consultation cabins can be placed to this zone.

Research and analysis wing can be placed in this zone. Use of white marbles, reduced plinths white colour, wooden organic panelling and silver articles with crystals will enhance the virtue of this zone. It can be a good zone for newborn babies. Underground water tanks, borewells should be in this zone of the plot. Do not grow big trees in this zone. A small fountain and water body will add sanctity and divinity to the space.

c. **East zone:** This zone is good for entrance lounge, reception, minor operations and OPD. This zone should be open so that Pranik streams will get easy circulation in the whole hospital. Do not provide any water body, storage and godowns in this zone. A form that opens out to east, has excellent pranik quality so terraces to east, c-opening to east, more site margin to east will create a better streaming and no toilets to this zone as they arrest the Prana. This zone represents fire element, so toilets in this zone will create wrong expression of 5 great elements. A closed east, a loaded east, east with toilets and staircase will lead to defamation and failure. Fire in east represents warmth so it gives general recovery to patients. Sky light in east will give continuous prana to the spaces. The deity of east is Aaditya so east streaming will give divine enclave to the organic activity of brain.

d. **Southeast zone:** This is the zone of power and strength. A physiotherapy unit, sonography, MMR, X-rays can be organised to this zone. Pantries, kitchens, small storage, ironing units, minor operation theatres, a medical shop, equipment of surgery can be organised to this zone. Use wooden floors, wooden panelling to walls in this zone.

Do not keep blood banks and blood storages in this zone. Storage of saline bottles and medicines are allowed in this zone. Main power connections, computer rooms, accounts, billing sections, transformers are allowed in this zone. This zone represents intense fire which has a quality of purification. Do not provide toilets and entrance in this zone. Do not use any red colour or red article in this zone. Toilets in this zone will disturb the equation and balance of fire element. Try to maintain this zone with raised plinth as compared to northwest, north, northeast and east zone. Do not provide any underground water tanks and borewells in this zone.

e. South zone. If this zone is loaded, it limits the negative energy. If this zone is dark, it limits the sun streams. Hence big machines related to hospitals, godowns, toilets, waste materials, systems like inverters, staircases are suitable for this zone. South streams represent hardship, pain and sorrow. So lesser the south stream, better is the cosmic equation of the space. This zone represents a command, force and strict administration. So cabins of management and executive authorities can be arranged in this zone. If long corridors are planned in this zone, then use of pyramidal roofs to the ceiling is necessary. Raised plinths, additional floors, yellow flooring, stone cladding, pyramidal ceiling, wooden floorings, heaviness thick plantation, towering structures are helpful to control the negative energy and pingala-sun streams.

f. Southwest zone: This is a zone of earth element, which represents all qualities of earth. Stability, fertility strength, yin effects are equated to the southwest zone. Due to earth qualities it arrests all types of streaming, so operation theatres and delivery rooms are specifically classified for this zone, so that excessive streaming of blood does not happen. Again all types of dry storages, operation theatres, closed and confined pattern, heavy machinery is suitable to this zone. Pyramidal roofs, raised floors, heavy landscape are suitable for this zone. Towering southwest assures great success, name and fame. Strictly any water body should not be arranged to southwest zone. As wind direction is predominantly from southwest to northeast, water zones may promote the travel of virus in the entire space. Never provide any duct or cut in this zone as loss of earth element leads to many disorders and malfunctioning. All bankrupt medical institutions have large open spaces and cuts in this zone. All unsuccessful doctors have clinics and hospitals with basements in southwest zone.

g. West zone. The seed deity, i.e. Ang-devta of west is friend or Mitra. If care is taken to control the Jambuk–Vikshep deity of west then the entire west zone acts like a friend with the owner. This could be a good zone for special rooms. Special rooms have attached toilets which match to the west zone. If west zones have ducts and open spaces to relative east zones, then these zones, though in west, get lot of Pranik energy. In such a case this becomes a good healing zone. Use blue glass to west side windows. Keep toilet and loads in west zone. Provide aluminium foil surface to west zone. For balconies towards west side, use blue tiles and bury lead metal below the floorings. Use of pyramidal ceiling in metal element will control the west streams, leading to loss of power of Jambuk. Less site margin to west with one Peepal tree at centre will increase the power of Aaditya-streams.

Overall, medical stores, godowns, refreshment, toilets, nurses quarters, retiring rooms will be the best arrangement for west zones.

h. Northwest zone. Due to contribution of north energy, this is a positive zone. Northwest along with southeast direction forms a wind-fire axis. West is a sunk zone but northwest does not represent sinking characters. Hence it can be used additional for pathological laboratories. This zone could support the work of research and analysis. Small classrooms, libraries and computers can be a good alternative for this zone. The deities of northwest are Rog, Rudra and Rudra Jay, so this can be a good healing zone. Additional facilities to patients like Pranayan (=breathing techniques), meditation and prayers are suitable to this zone. Department of psychiatry if allotted to this zone will give speedy recovery, if this zone is free of faults.

Case study- Hospital in Baramati

With all modern facilities and able doctors the unit is a complete failure. The architect is well-known and an experienced professional from Pune.

As shown in a block plan the structure represents a shape that opens out to south. Additional floors to north have blocked the organic streams. Basement to west zones is a sin in Vaastu principals. Thick plantation to north zone has blocked the positive energy. The basic rule that "west= high, east=low", "south=high and north=low" is not followed due to the form of the building. Common toilets are placed in northeast corner which is a crime in Vaastu principles. In India, architects feel excited using a Roman concepts, Western aspects and Islamic facades to the building, but they feel ashamed of using a traditional energy grid analysis of Vaastu Shastra.

It is a sign of servitude to imitate Western ideas and when they praise our culture then we feel elated and use Western concepts even more. A simple example of this bitter truth is the use of French windows in the tropical Indian country.

These French windows project the entire house to the scorching sun, so that radiation count in the environment increases the possibilities of malignancy and cancers. Fast-

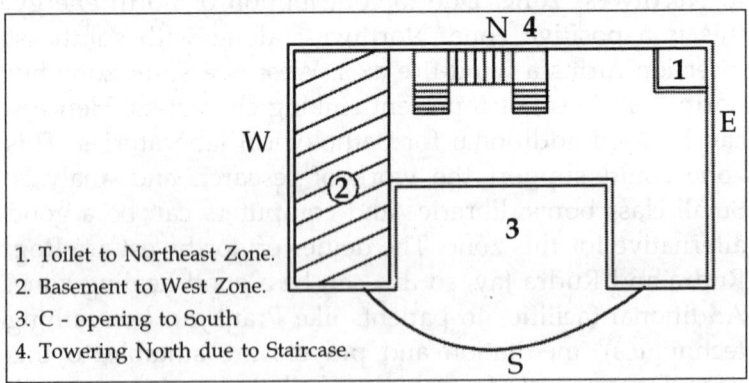

Figure 16

blowing winds carry lots of dust in the house leading to all types of allergies, asthma and skin diseases. Apart from Vaastu, simple climatology and environment constraint will also disallow the use of French windows. A traditional Jaipur window is a climate and environment friendly element which keeps the scorching sun away and reduces the wind effect.

17

Shops, Malls and Stores

Prices of commercial premises are so high that builders try to cover every inch under the shop. This greed for something more spoils the geometry of premises. Normally these odd shapes, projections, compulsory basements and compact planning disturb the energetics of the space. By all such cases, artificial streaming, lights and many other mediums play an important role. Balancing the zones and elements, circulating the light and sound, projecting the product and adorning

the available facades are multidimensional activities. Forms play an important role in balancing the energy in the space. Aggressive marketing is a common phenomenon in present day. This aggressive attack is not under the control of nine planets, it falls in the orbit of Neptune, Harshal and Pluto, which are the leaders of modern events and modern world. Neon signs, large crowds, shocking rhythms, ever changing ideas, Hide and seek mentality, involvement of huge wealth, lustrous shining surfaces and giant speed are actions of Neptune, Harshal and Pluto.. This being the period of these planets, one can see its reflections in every field of social life. People assemble in huge crowds like a flock of sheep to surrender their skills, intelligence and individuality to some Guru; unfortunately they are not the Jupitarian but Neptune and Pluto-oriented fancy Gurus. Coming to the point that since 9 planets are not effective in modern places like malls, multiplex and departmental shops, one should correlate the activity by Neptune, Harshal and Pluto to the zones and directions. Dance and volcanic presentation of energy should be done through the combination of opposite elements. Stroke explosion and miraculous exposure play important role in the marketing. A type of vulgarity with some shades of violence, along with non-ethical exposure are the key words in the modern aggressive advertising. Hence it becomes the play of opposite elements and different planets as mentioned above. Use of huge glass panels, 3-D light effects, loud sound, breaks and cuts are the key words in planning. With this respect, I will suggest following elemental expression for different zones and directions.

a. North zone: Provide multilevel lunar shapes with blue and white light effects in mirror forms. Use showers, sprinklers and fountains at various levels. Use traditional music with fusion of Western music in this zone. Use of fish ponds and golden turtles will create energy. All eatables, juices, ice creams deep freeze products, vegetables, silver and glass articles, crystals, female-oriented flashy articles, sweets, fruits, light weight things, chandeliers, bells, etc. can be arranged in the north zone.

b. East zone: Provide wooden panelling with light red and golden lights with few and light plantation. Green golden and little red colour enhance the virtue of east zone. Use copper metal in cladding the walls. Use of white marble with silver and copper inlays will exploit the qualities of east zone. White lights encased in walls and flooring will accelerate the Aaditya-streams or Prana in the space. This zone is under the control of Venus, sun and mars and is classified for Agni-Tatwa. Here the expression of fire is warmth and not the heat. All types of vegetables, wooden, silver and copper articles, jewellery related to red Coral, ruby and diamonds, male-oriented articles, small electrical items, cloths, medicinal herbs, light weight things, spices, dry fruits, etc. can be arranged in this zone.

c. South zone: Provide stone cladding, wooden panelling in combination of copper foils to this zone. Provide very little light from south or use yellow glass to windows. Use pyramidal yellow-coloured false ceiling to this zone. Heavy furniture, statues, non-vegetarian eatables, heavy weights and loads, steel and iron articles are suitable to this zone. Use of pyramidal roofs, loads and yellow colour will stabilize the earth element, absorb and dilute the negative energy of south zone.

d. West zone: This zone is represented by Saturn, Venus and mercury. Use metallic pyramids for the ceiling. Provide blue colour light effects. Use of stainless steel sheets or aluminium foil will enhance the virtues of west zone. Blue Crystals and blue glass will enhance the deity of west zone. Powerful western zones, accelerate the eastern streams. Juices, wines, glass articles, ladies wear, silverand metal articles, weapons, loads and heavy cabinets are suitable to this zone.

f. Sub-directions: These are the zones of combination of the adjoining main directions. Additional effects of five great elements are classified for each sub-direction. For example, southeast represents fire element, so for southeast zone one should use the combination of south and east zones along with effects of five great elements should be taken in to consideration.

Sample case study for shops

a. Shop with road to east

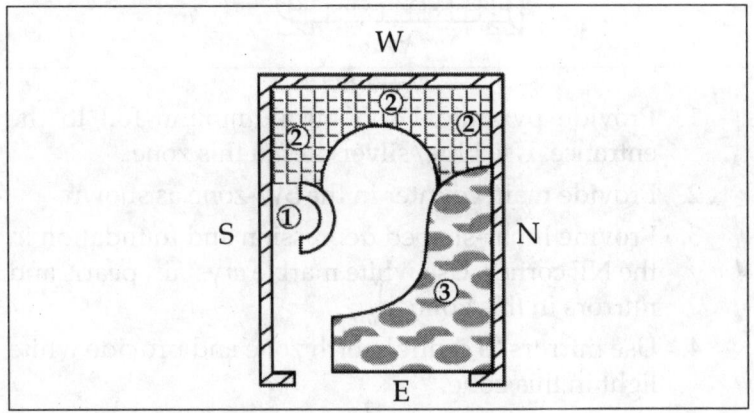

Figure 17

1. Place the counter in central south zone, facing north.
2. Provide the highest load in SE, S, SW and W zone as shaded.
3. Use White marble in N, NE and central east zone.
4. Create the depression in N, NE and east zone by taking pits in the plinth, but maintain the flooring level by using white marble.
5. May use wooden flooring to the enhance east zone.

b. Shop with road to west

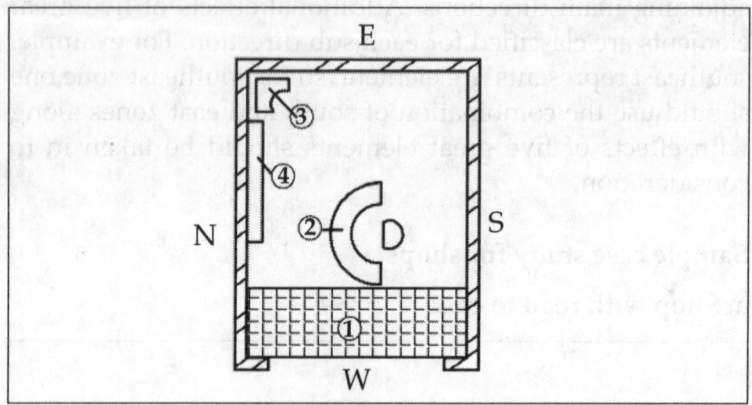

Figure 17.1

1. Provide pyramidal roof in aluminium foil to the entrance. Use blue/silver tiles in this zone.
2. Provide main counter in the SW-zone as shown.
3. Provide lunar-shaped depression and foundation in the NE corner. Use white marble crystals, pearls and mirrors in this zone.
4. Use mirrors to central north zone and provide white light in this zone.
5. Use stone cladding or heavy loads or wooden panelling to the south wall.

c. Shop with road to north

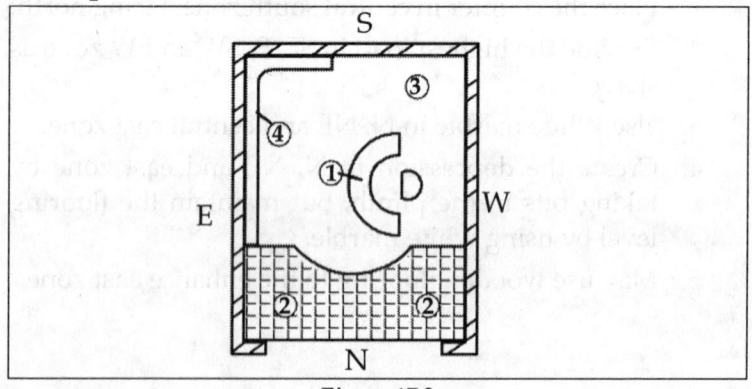

Figure 17.2

1. Place the main counter in the central west zone with face to the east.
2. Provide white marble in lunar shape to the enhance zone of North.
3. Use light weight material in the entrance zone and put max load towards S and W zones.
4. Use deodar wooden panelling to the central east wall up to the SE zone.
5. Use 2 steps to the plinth descending down to the north.

d. Shop with road to south
1. Provide pyramidal roof to the entrance zone. Use wood or yellow glass or stone for these pyramids.
2. Provide main counter facing east in the SW corner as shown.
3. Provide mirror fountain crystal, pearls and white marble assembly in the northeast corner

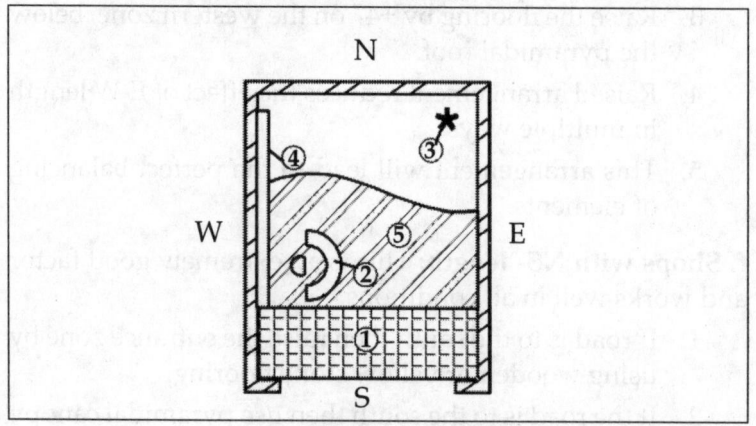

Figure 17.3

4. Provide metal toil panelling to the west NW zone of walls.
5. Use yellow colour flooring to entrance zone and white colour flooring to the inside part of the shop.

e. Shops with E-W length

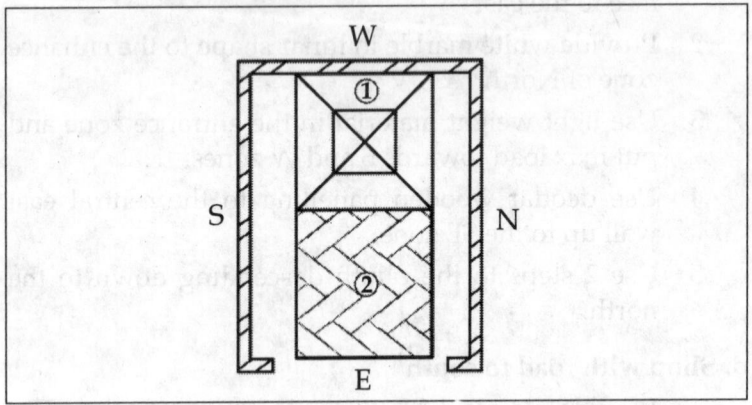

Figure 17.4

1. Use pyramidal roof in metal toil to the west zone and provide blue colour road flooring to this zone.
2. Use wooden flooring or white marble flooring to the east zone.
3. Raise the flooring by +4" on the western zone, below the pyramidal roof.
4. Raised arrangement reduces the effect of E-W length in multiple ways.
5. This arrangement will lead to the perfect balancing of elements.

f. Shops with NS- length: This is an extremely good factor and works well in all conditions.

1. If road is to the south then raise the entrance zone by using wooden or yellow stone flooring.
2. It the road is to the south then use pyramidal canopy in wood, stone or yellow glass
3. It road is to the north then use White marble flooring to the entrance zone.

4. If road is to the north then do not raise the southern part of the plinth.
5. It road is to the north then place the main counter to the west zone, facing east.
6. If the road is to the south, then place the main counter to the entrance SW-zone facing NE and E.

g. Shops with road to SW

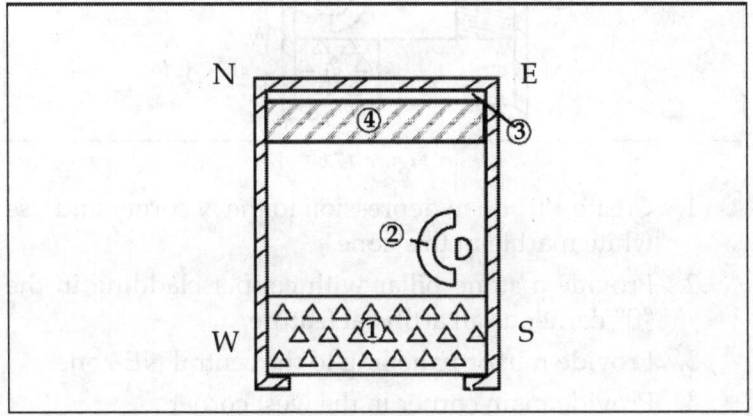

Figure 17.5

1. Provide pyramidal canopy to the entrance and apply golden or yellow colour. Use yellow tile flooring to entrance zone.
2. Provide main counter in south corner.
3. Provide mirror panelling to inner NE wall.
4. Create an artificial depression to NE zone as shown by the shaded area in drawing.
5. Provide white marble to inner side, towards NE zone. Raise the entrance zone by an additional plinth with yellow pattern flooring.

h. Shops with road to NW

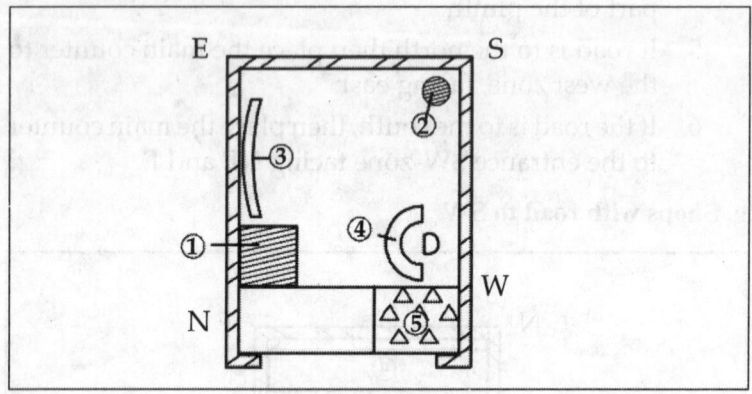

Figure 17.6

1. Create 3'0" deep depression to the N corner and use white marble in this zone.
2. Provide a stone pillar with copper cladding in the "S" corner as an artificial feature.
3. Provide mirror panelling to the central NE-zone.
4. Provide main corner in the west corner.
5. Use pyramidal canopy near the main counter with metallic foil.

i. Shops with road to SE

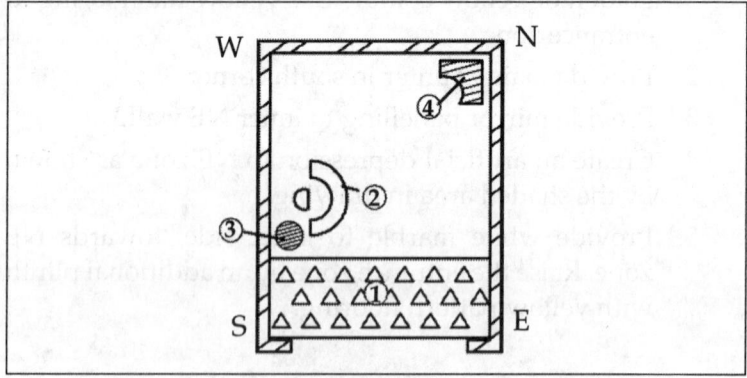

Figure 17.7

1. Provide pyramidal canopy to the entrance zone and give Silver colour to it.
2. Provide main corner in the "S" corner as shown.
3. Provide stone pillar in "S" corner as an artificial feature.
4. Provide lunar-shaped water body to the N corner with mirror panelling to the wall.
5. Raised the entrance zone by wooden flooring.

j. Shops with road to NE.

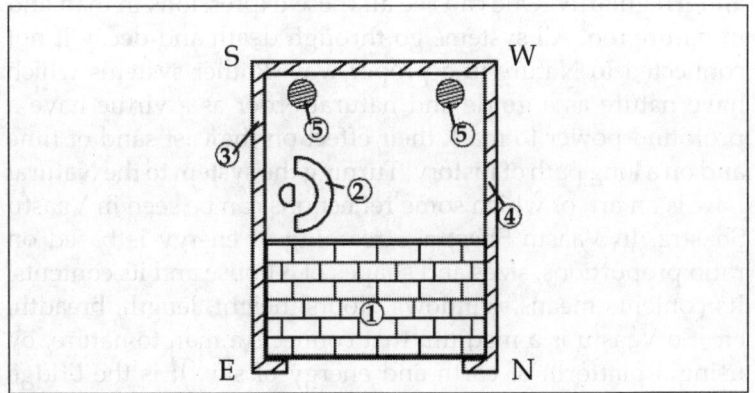

Figure 17.8

1. Provide white marble to the entrance zone.
2. Use the central SE area for the main counter.
3. Provide wooden panelling to the SE zone.
4. Provide metal panelling to the NW- wall.
5. Provide two pillars in the two inner most corners to create the load effect in SW- zone.

Conclusion

Modern days represent a period of hyperactivity, uncertainty and irregularity. One can see all these expressions in man and in nature too. All systems go through death and decay if not connected to Nature in a proper way. Rather systems which have nature as a guide and natural order as a virtue have a profound power to mark their effect on the vast sand of time and on a long path of history. Turning the system to the Natural Law is an art, of which some reflections can be seen in Vaastu Shastra. In Vaastu Shastra, streaming of energy is based on ratio proportions, sizes and shapes of a house and its contents. Its contents means, windows, doors, height, length, breadth, etc. So Vaastu is a medium that connects a man to nature, by using a platform of earth and energy of sky. It is the bridge that connects the inner space of being and vast outer expanse of nature. Vaastu is like a Yantra in three dimensions where energy forms of deities protect the being, enrich the becoming and enhance the experience of life. The entire Western world has given great importance to the art of administration and management of events, so practically one can see that this subject is overpowering to the real basic scientific world. Whereas the tradition of Eastern scholars has focussed their attention on the creation of positive events and improvement of the virtuous dimensions of life. Vaastu, yoga, astrology, music and Ayurveda are the 5 sub-branches of great ascetic tradition of the Eastern world. Chakrakar or Mandalacar, i.e. helical streaming of energy is one of the principles of this ascetic tradition. Reflection of nature in human being and extension of human existence in nature are the two important focus points in all enquiries. So that one compatible platform for man and nature creates a right relationship in Man and Nature.

Vibrations, waves, sound and light are the four parameters that create the quality of organic living experience in the matter. This connectivity of energy and matter, soul and body, sky and earth is the principal theme of Vaastu, yoga, astrology, music and Ayurveda.

Comprehensive perception and all-pervading existence are two main pointers to know the Eastern stream of thought. It is easy to formulate the norms of discipline because the factors are quite static in nature. But these oriental sciences are aimed to attain the order and virtue of Nature, which are supersensitive and megadynamic in nature.

When violence is grasping the social order more in the Western world and poverty is dominating the social discipline more in the Eastern world, probably these oriental sciences with ascetic tradition and austerity could be the only hope to maintain human element in this universe. They create well-being, healthy life, ordered behaviour and a peaceful surrounding that is the purpose of oriental sciences. Eastern traditional scholars have given a key to peace, prosperity and progress through observation of Nature and mankind. Any process which has least friction, less blockage and low impedance lasts long. This fine tuning of being with the Natures is the central theme of oriental sciences. Rhythm is a local phenomenon. Frequency is a global phenomenon and synchronicity is a connecting phenomenon. Oriental sciences speak of this synchronicity, i.e. a dynamics of being and becoming.

This book is devoted to the study of industrial and commercial premises with traditional thought of Vaastu Shastra and feng shui. The author hopes that this writing will help to enhance the perception of ancient scientific and logical knowledge of India.

Credits

In this book I have just made an attempt to correlate the thoughts of some renowned sages and scholars of the subject.

I give credit for this book to them; without their blessings and inspiration, it would have been an arduous task to cover this vast subject.

I express my sincerest thanks and gratitude to – Dr. R. N. Shukla (Scientist), Dr. Sunanda Rathi (Astrloger), Dr. Mehar Master Moos (Global Healer), Aum Chintamani Mudholkar, Shri. Sripad Mitkar (Sage and Scholar), Shri. Shivmuni Maharaj (Jainacharya), Sant Sri Malhari Baba (Chandrapur), Sri Krishna Chaitanya (Sai KaKa).

Tips

The great failure of Enron is an accurate example of faulty soil and zone. The land of Dabhol has sea to south/southwest/west zone. Even to some southeast parts nearer to the project, there is a deep sea coast. Whenever the land slopes to the south, southwest and west zone, the pingala streams attack the entire zone, leading to all calamities which can be explained as death, destruction, demolition, discontinuity and defamation. 'Probably all' these five bitter experiences are tested by government body. At least where huge investments are concerned, government should respect our traditional science by following some minimum constraints as explained in the theory.

The business market and industries show some fantastic irregularities regarding growths and profits to some product, like some temporary comets in the sky. In short duration the comet starts dissolving the aura and spread becomes a flashy soil. Many times one can read such events through their symbols. The symbol of "Satyam" has a vertical cobra-like ascend but has a dissipating void at the bottom representing a baseless growth.

In examples like "Satyam" the basic shape of the building shows the deceit and wrong cultures. All such places have north-south length with lot of aggression of west represented by "C" shape. The deity of west is Varun (Harshal) and has vices, like unpredictable behaviour and false presentation, which ultimately leads to disagreement in every walk of life

Flashy fluorescent colours and neon sign-lights create the voids, where Rahu rules. Rahu is the king of the present period as Rahu represents the polluted poisonous orbit of wind element. The mall culture in the present time is based on this fluorescent lights and neon signs, where a new negative revolution is breaking the divine orders of Jupiter, Venus and moon. Even good business and good products are forced to follow these techniques for better survival.

Why are Chitale in Pune, Hafeez Contractor in Mumbai and Norman Foster in London successful? They have a correct form and right relationship to the light. Excitation of north and reloading the south is the most popular slogan of Vaastu, if followed correctly then there are chances to become Chitale, Hafeez and Norman Foster. Chitale Sweet Mart has road to north and east with lunar shape to northeast. Travel of light is from north to south and east to west, i.e. from source to sink. Lunar shape to northeast means a matter of form, water is to northeast. Northeast streaming leads to divinity and monopoly. Large number of people in Pune use sweets of Chitale as the *naivedya* or offering to their beloved deities.

The office place of the great architect Hafeez Contractor in Mumbai is L-shaped that opens out to northeast zone. The southern limb of "L" is at higher level (Satisfying the law of Vaastu as south=high and north= Low). The western limb of the space is at lower level. This zone has double height, means northern air column is powerful and southern earth element is established. In traditional language this shape is called as Dakshin Pashchim Dvishala. "One who operates through such a form, becomes a king or monopolist in the business." This prophecy of shastra and Hafeez's esteem in the market are matching the practical events.

One simple remedy to reduce the effect of sun streams is to reload the south, southwest and west zone. Hence in the main cabin of the chairman keep 50 kg lead pyramid of golden colour to southwest zone, 35 kg lead pyramid of yellow colour to south zone and 15kg lead pyramid of blue/silver colour to west zone. This ratio proportion of heavy lead metal will do the contraction of the Vikat, Putana and Jambuk the Vikshep deities of south, southwest and west. Just one remedy is enough to create a virtuous change in the cosmic energy.

If in some factory, roof slopes are to south and west, then this disturbs the thermal equation, creating imbalance in the bio-magnetism attached to it. Entire energetics of the factory gets disturbed. Multiple folds of anticlockwise loops of negative energy kill the main deities in the Vaastu Purusha Mandal. This high thermal torque creates the panic in the aspirations and zones. In such case a tremendous rise in the quantity and content of the earth element in south/southwest/west zone is absolutely essential to improve the condition of the factory. After this correction relocate the transparent sheets in roof in the relative north and east zone, so that travel of light from source zone can stabilize the positive deities of the Vaastu Purusha Mandal.

When the purpose of the form is entertainment, gambling, prostitution, financial transaction, immoral freedom, bars and all types of non-vegetarian foods then the excitation of west plays an important role. Varun and Jambuk deities are supportive to all the above characters. Normally all such spaces have prolonged working hours and flooding of people after the sunset, when the power of west starts ruling the sky. Clubs, hotels and discotheques are counter-places and alternatives to the 7th house in the horoscopes. Even structures like "C" opening to west, i.e. Varun-Choola also gives a fantastic result for such purpose. Activation of northwest also plays an important role in such activities.

Energy, matter, elements, aspirations and the form play important roles in the success of any structure. Either of the three constraints mentioned above should be positive for a minimum level of the appreciation of the space. In any industrial structure, it is easy to rectify the "energy-matter equations" by readjusting the light in the spaces and by creating artificial depressions in the surroundings. A grace of element can be carried in the space by using different shapes and colours. If proper thought is given, without major changes in machinery layouts, one can artistically play to create the vibrant spaces.

The subject has crossed the bounds and limits of basic nine planets. Moreover it is in the zone of Harshal and Neptune, which are on the outer orbit of Solar System. These planets have less affinity and lesser control of sun, but they carry the miracles of vast outer sky. The present market reflects the volatile characters, hidden virtues and unknown controls of Harshal and Neptune.

All the religions mention the negative energy and events related to black magic. In the context of Vaastu Shastra, to protect the self and the spaces of our office/house/factory, various remedies are given that can be explained in the classical language as Kavach (shield), Argala (propagation of energy) and *Keelak* (nailing the negative spirits). The activity of Kavach is related to the deity "Brahma". The activity of Argala is related to the deity Vishnu and the activity of Keelak is related to the deity Shiva. All these rituals when performed in Vaastu they create the vibration and rhythm of A-U-M, i.e. pranava or helical streaming or mandalacar form of energy. Rightly said by Saint Dnyaneshwara, " Pranancha pranauchi karava ". In other words, transform the energy to travel in a mandalacar way: this happens when Vaastu undergoes the rituals related to Kavach, Argala and Keelak.

If in some factory, the load of machinery lies in the north zone and comparatively south is empty then, a) Create depressions to the north-northeast zones of plots. b) Provide transparent sheets in the roof to the north zone. c) Reload the empty south zone by stones to raise the plinth level. d) Paint the south zone of roof using yellow/brown/black colour. e) Limit the light and ventilation from south zone. f) Provide towering pyramidal roofs to the south zones. g) Provide boreholes to north/northeast zones wherever possible.

Economy and financial constraints of one nation dictate the market and index of all the nations. One nation's economy depends on weapons and wars. One nation's economy falls due to hyper luxury and irresponsible expensive behaviour of citizens in that nation leading to collapse of many financial institutes. This creates the thirst, hunger and droughts in many other nations. All these events reflect the violence of Rahu, terminating behaviour of Harshal, mass suicide of Neptune and death of many comets.

In Mahad industrial estate, 50 km away from Mumbai, there are around 100 small-scale industrial units, out of which 75 units are closed. A huge investment is wasted due to non-functioning. The exorbitantly high costing machinery of has been rusting away for the last many years. This total zone has a mountain range to north/northeast/east, and the nalla or the water zone is to south/southwest/west. Such a situation means imbalance of "energy matter equation", loss of power of five great elements, multiple anticlockwise loops of negative energy creating a malefic situation. In Indian architecture based on Vaastu Shastra there exist wonderful cosmic laws to select the land. If due respect is given to the minimum level it can save such huge financial losses.

Security, safety and sensitivity are the main problems of the modern world. Voids, violence and vulgarity are the important issues confronting everybody. Rhythm, synchronicity and frequency are the only answers to all the above problems and issues. The map of the world and balance of earth is totally disturbed. Due to the drift of land, north is loaded by the earth element. South is getting excited by the majority of water element. Axis of the earth is falling every 1000 years. This has changed the seasons, thermal constitution and global warming. In such a situation only Indian style of architecture speaks of mystique relation of nature and mankind through different deities, energy forms and sun. To tackle and reduce the criminal behaviour this branch of Vedic wisdom speaks on forms, elements, directions and aspirations.

No other system of architecture in the world has explicitly spoken on vibration, waves, sound and light with its organic relationship with human life. How to subtract the noise and how to create the sound that sounds positive energy is the basic theme in Vaastu Shastra by creating right proportions, sacred cuts and placement of elements in right zones. The right relationship to light leads to enlightenment and bio-rhythm which is the core of all the discussions of the oriental philosophy. The foundation of Vaastu Shastra is Vaastu Purusha Mandal which speaks of different deities that are different stages of sun, i.e. light source.

The treatment "Kavach" or a shield is a ritual called "Vaastu nabhi". In the southwest zone of the central Brahma part of the plot, this riutal is performed, along with the southeast column as the first auspicious act on the plot. Southeast column is called the "Agneya Sthambh". In this ritual on an auspicious time (muhurath) a 6' x 6' x 6' pit is refilled with a SHANKU at the centre by using river boulders. This high density zone in the Brahma, forces the energy to travel in a mandalacar way. Since this *nabhi*-node is eccentric and non-symmetric on the plot, with this node as the dynamic centre, or as the pivot point, the streaming of energy begins around it. This node classifies 5 divisions to water element and 4 divisions to all other elements; in a way it gives more importance to water element which supports the streaming.

Yog Vasishth, which is one of the oldest text on spiritualism, has defined "Vaastu Tatva" as Satta samanyam akhilam vastutatvam ehochyate . Here the first word, "Satta" means the order of nature. "Samanyam" means "that merges with the fact" and reality; "Akhilam" means that which is "omnipotent". That which contains all these three dimensions, there exist the Vaastu element. This means all that reflects the order of nature and merges with the nature and exists irrespective of all odds is called Vaastu. Hence, the home, factory or office, so far the container, contents and coordination match the time and direction, they will reflect the positive energy and progressive momentum.

All different styles of architecture have taken account of the climate, environment, use of local materials, solar path, etc., but nobody except Vaastu Shastra, i.e. Indian style of architecture has taken keen interest to know the relation of time and directions, the house and eventology of the life, dynamics of cosmic forces and mandalacar — helical streaming of energy. Mysticism of nature and its connectivity to different forms of energy are very nicely dealt in this subject through different deities and their correct placement, alignment and sensitivity. No other system of architecture has taken the role of earth and its contribution in the human life except the Vaastu Shastra. Rather Vaastu Shastra is considered as the science that creates right expression of all the five great elements.

One yellow-coloured pyramid in lead metal to south and one golden-coloured lead pyramid to southwest zone is a magic remedy to equalise the energy matter equation of Vaastu. A solid stable earth element emerges in the south and southwest zone due to these pyramids, so that moon streams from north/northeast zone get accelerated power to reach south/southwest zone, through a helical path. Yellow colour represents the stability of the earth element, whereas golden colour represents the yang, prosperous, generative component of the earth element. So by colour, shape, metal and pyramid as the medium, a virtuous and qualitative earth element emerges in the proper zone.

All the architectural colleges and syllabus contain studies of Islamic architecture, Gothic architectures or Roman style. It is unfortunate that there is no space for a subject like Vaastu in the universities and colleges. This subject is so comprehensive, relevant and beneficial in nature that it covers the environmental aspect, use of local materials, cosmic comprehensive laws of nature, connectivity of man and nature, etc. Through its parameters this science creates the energy continuum and protective shield so that the personal and cosmic breath are tuned to attain positive energy. Multiple dimensions of this science propagate a positive energy, which leads to positive events in life.

Effortless gain and torture less easy progress are the blessings of Vaastu. The huge new construction in Prati Shirdi of Annachhatra is a remarkable construction based on Vaastu Shastra and designed by me. The purpose of this place is to feed the devotees, i.e. tranquilising the fire of hunger. A divine form of "fire" a flame lies in the east zone so to get the bliss of divine fire. This structure is made with a form that opens out to east, i.e. "C" opening to east, traditionally called as "Aaditya-Choola". The kitchen is placed in SE-zone and the structure has north-south length. Relative south, southwest and west are raised by construction of magnificent domes. This monumental building has an age-old well to the north zone. All the elements are balanced. Form of the structure is matching to the purpose. Energy streaming is helical. This huge structure got built hardly in a period of 18 months.

The world famous Yoga authority BKS Iyengar's yoga institute in Pune is a marvellous example of Vaastu shashtra. His movement is connected to transformation of personal breath to the virtue of Jal-Tatwa or water elements. His yoga institute has a lunar/crescent shape which represents water element. This lunar shape opens out to north, with a good site margin to north. The structure has slope to north. On every floor all north facade has huge windows. Enhancement of the north flux and loaded southern zone can be observed in all these cases.

Norman Foster is considered as the Architect of this Century, whose work is being recognised globally. Hundreds of architects work under one roof and under his guidance in London. During my lecture in his office, the following Vaastu tenets were observed. His office can be considered a unique example of correct form, right relation with light and a perfect land, i.e. earth support. This location has a river to north. The famous Thames river being on the north zone, the zone is totally enhanced, leading to peace, prosperity and progress. His office has a complete glass facade which enables the north light in the whole office. The double height to north zone has enhanced the virtue of north, whereas single height to south has showered the virtue of earth element. The east-west length to the office has given variety of jobs, e.g., from stadiums to malls and from airport to commercial premises.

In the case of TAJ in Mumbai, till there was no load and no obstruction due to the extension of a high-rise building to "north", the structure enjoyed the voids and spaces of Rahu, Varun and Nights. The esteem as the "great entertainer and place for the business transactions" was beyond the limits. This structure is a Varun-Choola with "C" opening to west. Traditionally the west zone is called as "Rangshala" where

Venus also plays an important role. When north got loaded and first time the Saturn came in Leo sign, "all the faults around" gathered the negative momentum and the structure exploded on 26/11.

In all such storms and calamities, these structures which have a perfect form, right surroundings and balanced five great elements will survive with less friction, little blockage and reduced impedance due to a correct cosmic streaming. Aditya-Choola, structures with "C" opening to east; Som-Choola, structures with "C" opening to north; Dakshin-Pashchim Dvishala, L opening to NE and north-south length to the units are some conformed successful forms sanctioned by theory and practice both.

The word Keelak means nailing the carriers of negative energy on the boundary and avoiding their pollution and infections in the main energy zone. Reference of negative energy comes in all the religions with various forms as black magic, evil eyes, vortex, etc. In practical case studies, it has been observed that if form of the space is correct and Kavach/Argala and Keelak rituals are performed then the shield of that space becomes so powerful that the black magic does not work on such places. The ritual Keelak includes encasing lead rods in south walls/southwest walls and 7 brass rods in the west walls. If the entry is not from south or west then bury 9 steel rods 5'-0" long to south site margin and bury 7 steel rods 5'-0" long to west site margin. This ritual reduces the negative power of Vikat, Putana and Jambuk, which are Vikshep deities of S/SW/W for south zone, we can use the square geometry for burying these rods. For west zone, we can use the circle geometry for burying these rods.

Kamika-Aagam, one of the oldest text on Vaastu Shastra, has defined Vaastu as the super science and super technique.

In all the spiritual techniques, the movement related to Shiva and Maya is denied. In all the worldly movements the Shiva is denied and whole play is related to Maya. Vaastu is a super technique as it gives equal importance to the Shiva and Shakti, i.e. Maya. In Vaastu, elements represent the Shiva whereas streaming of energy is the play of Shakti, i.e. Maya. Interdependence of energy and elements is the theme of Vaastu Shastra. Many times there is a change of role of both entities. This change of roles makes Vaastu as a mystique subject. Right excitation of elements supports the streaming of energy whereas unless there is correct streaming on a helical path, elements do not emerge with full strength. This understanding of interdependence of two dimensions, two entities is deeply followed in all the processes of Vaastu Shastra.

The ideal zone for the main cabin is always in the south or southwest zone with face of the main person to north. The second important feature is that this zone should get the distant north light which represents the flowering of distant remote possibilities. The side marble with lunar shape and the side table should have black/brown or yellow colour top. Such cabins don't have any north or east light then this south/southeast earth element makes it dull, idle and diseased. So along with zone, the streaming of energy has equal importance.

In many factories, it is not possible to change the roofs or machinery layouts, positions of boilers, high-lows of the land, or zones of the buildings. In such a situation, if the main cabin of the chairman, vice-chairman or director is rectified on the principles of Vaastu, then often miracles happen and they experience a radical change in the market possibilities. The ideal proportion of a cabin is in the "golden ratio with north-south as the length". Distant clear north light is like an assurance of a success. If such light is not available then try to provide a sky light in the north zone. White marble flooring to relative north and east, along with Jaisalmer yellow stone flooring to relative south and southwest zone, assures the elements and energy streaming. Stone cladding to south, southwest walls, gives virtues of the earth element. One solid gold plated lead pyramid in southwest corner assures the complete balance of energy matter equation.

The renowned computer scholar and scientist Dr. Vijay Bhatkar's office cabin is a wonderful reflection of principles of Vaastu. In the total office premises his placement is in the central south zone, with light energy from north and east directions. The cabin has white marble flooring to the adjoining north and east zone. This cabin has yellow-coloured flooring and south/west walls have stone cladding. The yellow colour represents the fertile earth element where tradition and modernity both have equal balance. Black colour represents the distress of earth element, whereas brown colour represents the hardship of earth element. This cabin has "north-south length" which adds virtue to the organic stream. The table top was suggested in white marble with slight lunar shape to the north external face.

There was a charismatic era of Harshad Mehta in the world of finance. His suicidal courage, alert, clever mind, grip on the market was outstanding. It is interesting to study the house of such a dangerous, criminal and mastermind. The sea coast to south/southwest/west zone to his house reflects the tiger on which he was riding. Since north to his house was closed and loaded due to the staircase, so no positive outcome happened in his life. It was a duplex flat with reducing floor from south/SE zone, leading terraces to south/southeast zone. Excessive attack of pingala/sun streams of south/southwest/southeast created a suicidal fire in his personality. A cooling water element of north being absent, the fire got extended to explosion and his mystique death.

The treatment "KAVACH" includes fixation of deities, planets and elements. This is achieved by a ritual called as "Ratnadhyay". It is a mystique ritual connected to deities, aura and particular zones of the plinth. The auspicious stone acts as a yang seed implanted in the yin body of the earth in a way it acts as the "Tai-Chi", i.e. complete balance of zone, aspiration and elements. A correct placement of auspicious stones limits the boundaries of a plot and the vast sky energy starts radiating in the virtues of earth through the medium of directions. It is the miniature reflection of the solar system in the limited grid of the house. It is the ritual that connects and relates the microcosm of the house to the macrocosm of solar system. This ritual demarcates the energy channels and Sutra Devta in Vaastu.

Whenever light travels from "north to south" or "east to west" it reinforces the virtue and quality of the entire space. When proper elements are established in the zones, it leads to stability and right momentum in the space. So, a simple remedy is to provide transparent sheets in roof in the N and E zone of any factory. This simple correction will create the streaming from N to S and E to W, i.e. from source to sink. A second simple correction in the factory shed could be to apply blue colour to the west zone and yellow colour to the south zone of the roof.

It is the science that transforms the voids into spaces. It feels the gap between the cup and leaps, so that in life one enjoys the comfort, creativity and connectivity to the free will and blissful choice. By balancing the five great elements, it creates the aura of balanced planets around the person and house, so that oneness of mind and intelligence always leads to right action in life. Tuning of breath, unification of mind and intelligence and right choices in life being the real gift of this science so this science is called as *Sthapaty-Veda*.

The word *Argala* is connected to the energy that gives prosperity. Hence all the rituals related to north zone means presenting Argala or the energy to the space. The element of north is water that spreads as the prosperity. By allotting one extra division to Jal tatva in Nabhi ritual, the process of Argala begins. Virtues of water element are expressed with pearls, crystal, silver, white light, depression, lunar shape, mirror and white marble. Whenever light falls on the water face, light gets polarised. Crystals and white marble have the same virtue of polarising the light. Whenever all the above characters get clubbed to north zone, to create the source element in the north direction, the ritual of Argala gets completed. It is preferable to do all north corrections on Monday morning as the Muhuratha or the most auspicious time.

Hence poison of Rahu, eccentric behaviour of Harshal, mass hypnotism of Neptune and short rising and fast diminishing comets rule the present time and sky. Monstrous lust, naked humans, voids and strokes, all types of irregularities, eccentric shapes and colours, rat race and immoral acts will dictate the world of advertising, media and architecture.

Grid planning is the base of Architecture, whereas dynamic energy grid planning is the base of Indian style of Architecture, i.e. Vaastu Shastra. In modern science the reference of Kari Grid or Heartman's grid of bioenergy is given. This concept has been considered in a much better way in Vaastu Shastra. The whole plot is divided in 9 x 9, i.e. 81 divisions. Each division is separated by a stream of energy of L/72 or B/72. These energy channels are kept free of any column and beam positions, so that the earth's bioenergy is forced to travel in the order and discipline of the house. In traditional Vaastu these are termed as Sutra-Devta, viz. Kamala, Sati, Savita, Pranvahini, etc., around the Vaastu Purusha Mandala. A profound, immense and intense energy of nature is channelize to stream in the house in a mandalacar form so that home becomes a perfect shield.

In case of Kirloskar pneumatics, the factory shed had too many obstructions on the path of the energy. Many mezzanines of multiple levels created a mess in the streaming, light and ventilation. Though the shed had a north-south length, the effective area never represented any order and discipline. The entire north zone was raised loaded and shabby so though the north was open, energy was absent. In such cases just cleansing the paths of energy creates a virtue in the space, which leads to progress and prosperity. Some mezzanines were dismantled to clear the flow of energy. Some old machines were removed from the working zone. Huge openings to north and east started pouring the organic and pranik energy. Transparent sheets in north and east zone gave a positive aura to the whole space. Just regulating the energy stream played a fantastic role in the creativity, production and discipline

Mumbai's Chhatrapati Shivaji International Airport has a unique shape which assures a good peace in the present period of turbulence. It has a crescent lunar shape that opens out to north. Water represents streaming and movement. When water is channelized it leads to a discipline, order and forward movement. This airport is the busiest airport of India and highest movement is observed in this Vaastu. If at all any violence happens (violence means fire) due to tranquilising water shape, this violence will subside and will not lead to any huge losses. In addition if 9 flags get erected to the south zone and a huge water body is planned in the northern zone/ entrance zone, then this Vaastu format assures the peace, prosperity and progress.

Simple remedies for industries, in which one need not do any change inside the factories is of prime importance, as it doesn't indulge in the day-to-day routine—a) Provide nine borewells in a lunar geometry to the north and northeast zone. b) Provide nine mounts in landscape to the south zone. c) Plant nine Christmas trees/Almond trees to the south zone d) Erect nine golden/yellow colour flags to south zone. e) Provide pyramidal structures to south zone. f) Keep all garbage load, steel racks to south zone g) Bury lead/steel metal to south zone h) Paint yellow colour on south sloping roofs. i) Provide transparent sheets to the north slope. j) Provide circular white marble pieces to north zone. k) Provide lunar-shaped water bodies to north zone and do the finishing in white marble. l) Shift the big plants of north zone to southside m) If any machines, clarifiers or huge cylinders are in north zone then at least paint them in white or silver colour.

Amidst the "future and the present" there lies a form and a space. If form has dynamic symmetry and space has no voids then the future is brighter than the present. If form has no order and spaces have dark shades of voids then the future is dreadful and present is in danger. Vaastu gives a compatible form to the nature and refills the voids by energy to transform them in the spaces. In the oriental tradition this sense of direction and presence of time have been clubbed by single connotation *Dik-Kal* where *dik* means direction that defines the quality of *Kal*, i.e. time. "Space–time as a continuum" filled by "quantum energy" defines the existence and is the basis of oriental philosophy. Whenever north gets blocked, it reduces the spaces and the form gets disturbed. Whenever south gets excited, it disturbs the form and voids get activated. The massacre of 9/11 has the same background. There were two towers, north tower being higher than south tower, it created obstruction in the energy streaming. south/southwest/ southeast zone to the adjoining part of the two towers of WTC is having a deep coastal depression and excitation of Pingala/ sun streams of south/southwest/west, which leads to death, destruction, defamation, discontinuity and deletion. The entire north–south axis being disturbed, when the cosmic north got disturbed and polluted then the event happened.

The success story of Mr. H. R. Gaikwad, the chairperson of Bharat Vikas Group, is interesting. He is an obedient follower of the principles of Vaastu. He removed the asymmetric zones of his house and relocated the house with "L" shape that spread out to the NE zone. Borewell, sleeping zone, kitchen, windows and every possible element is relocated in the house. In office the entrance correction by pyramidal canopy, metal treatment, Ratnadhyaya was done. His cabin has north-south length with proportion of the golden ration. In cabin, light flux is only from N and E zones. Mr. Gaikwad faces north with a table top of white marble and to the left in SW corner loads of lead pyramid curtails the negative energy. The progress of Mr. Gaikwad and his graph of rise in the market is vertical and ascending.

In a big industrial set up, if some 2/3 structures are planned to follow the Vaastu tenets, then the virtue of these spaces will take care of many anomalies in the surroundings. If all important jobs, like research and development, accounts and sales, main chairman's, director's cabin are kept in this zone, then these leaders can change the future of that industry. All such structures should have any of these four shapes that have proved their excellence. a) C opening to east is called as the Aaditya-Choola. This structure leads to discipline in working, vitality in research and honesty in behaviour. b) C opening to north is called as the Uttar-Choola. This structure leads to prosperity and abundance and general creativity in the development and fame in the market. c) L opening to northeast is called Dakshin-Pashchim- Dvishala. This structure leads to effortless gain, unique position in the market and monopoly in the product. d) Towering pyramidal roof to south and west along with sloping roof to north and east can be named as Shivling Kruti which is a perfect cosmic form.

•••